THE BOOK OF MEMES

THE BOOK OF MEMES

An Engineers Model of Life, the Universe, and Everything

STEVE MONIZ

LIBERTY HILL PUBLISHING

Liberty Hill Publishing
555 Winderley Pl, Suite 225
Maitland, FL 32751
407.339.4217
www.libertyhillpublishing.com

Paperback ISBN-13: 979-8-86850-692-5
Ebook ISBN-13: 979-8-86850-693-2

Dedication

My model of *How the World Works* merges the concepts of a select few of history's great thinkers. These are the Prophets and higher in my personal pantheon.

Saint Roddenberry is honored for his positive vision of humanity, where the goal of civilization is to enable all individuals to achieve their maximum potential.

My Muses are William Shakespeare, Isaac Newton, Charles Darwin, and Douglas Adams. From them comes my model of Life, the Universe, and Everything.

My focus on complexity/chaos theory was inspired by the Agents of Chaos: Ilya Prigogine, Edward Lorenz, James Gleick, and Norman Packard. May their names not be forgotten.

And all praise to Gaea, Goddess of Complexity, who commanded, "If things can get more interesting, they will."

Table of Contents

Introduction

This book describes my *model* of how the universe works, given a sample size of one planet. It includes physics from Shakespeare to Adams and the relatively new discipline of *complexity theory*. It has saints and sinners, rebels and causes. It explores history and human interactions in the context of *memes* and the *tribes* humans have developed over the ages.

Memes for the Ages

Memes as a culture transmission device – They're not just funny GIFs.

The memes here aren't those cleverly captioned pictures from the internet. These memes are what *Sage* Richard Dawkins meant when he coined the word "meme" in *The Selfish Gene* in 1976. Memes are to societies/tribes/cultures what genes are to species; they transmit *information* down the time stream. Memes are the ideas that define our cultures. Song and dance and hats are visible cultural clues and part of the *bonding* memes that keep the tribe together. Techno-memes made us rich. Here we cover *behavioral* memes–how humans *interact* with each other.

The Great Memes changed history (twice).

The Great Memes are two behavioral *suggestions* that changed the course of human history. (All memes are merely suggestions. They're more what you'd call guidelines than actual rules.[1]) The two Great Memes are the *Barbarian* meme and the *Trust* meme. The Great Memes divide human history into three Ages: the Stone Age, the Age of Empire, and our current Age of Plenty.

Alternative set of historical Ages

The "standard" Ages of Man are the Stone, Agricultural, and Industrial ages. *alt.ages* is the faux Usenet title for my alternative list. The alt.age.tribes chart also shows the major types of human *Tribe* that have emerged over the ages.

---

1 ref Cpt. Barbossa @*BlackPearl*

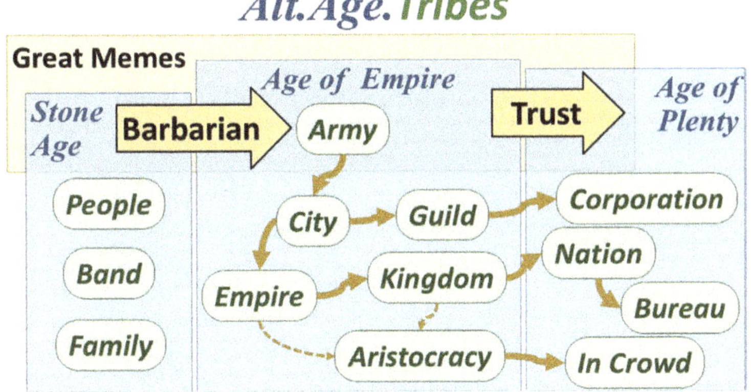

Memes for the Ages

Major Tribes of Man

The alt.ages of human societies began about 50,000, 5,000, and 500 years ago, for those of you fond of logarithmic scaling. The transition from the Stone Age to Age of Empire was triggered by the Barbarian meme which emerged from the Agriculture (Ag)[2] meme which itself emerged about 10,000 years ago. The Trust meme ushered in our current Age of Plenty. Both Great Memes[3] are based on interactions between tribes. Barbarians treated their neighbors rather badly. We do better now with

[2] Named memes are in caps.

[3] Catch Phrases, some in the public domain, are capitalized.

respect to our neighbors and trust our own people more with our democratic memes.

Tribes

Tribalism for fun and profit

The tribes highlighted above are the most important ways humanity has organized itself since coming down from the trees. We were apes then and had just *Band* and *Family* as our tribes. Scholars usually credit language for creating "humanity." Language united bands into the largest "natural" human tribe, the *People*. Interactions between the peoples of Earth supplies most written history. All tribes have a *culture*, including lore and memes for how to behave within the tribe, plus xeno-memes for dealing with other tribes. Tribes have a *Social Contract*, in which the individual members have *duties*. You give up some freedom to obtain the benefits of belonging to the tribe. That's the deal.

Do you know your Tribes?

Humans choose their tribes. How many do you have? Which are most important? How are they treating you? How do they treat other tribes? Are they (still) offering a good deal? Have they strayed from the path that made them worthwhile? It would behoove the reader to take an inventory of their tribes and examine their status within each. Get to know your tribes and be aware of others. They're all over the place.

Complexity

The third major theory of 20th century physics

Physics before the 20th century was Newtonian. The first two paradigm shifts of modern physics were relativity and quantum mechanics. Scholars have designated complexity theory as the third great paradigm shift in 20th century physics. It is admittedly a distant third. Complexity theory covers fractals and self-replicating structures and artificial life, but the focus here is on (complex) *evolving systems*. The weather is a "dumb" complex system. But even dumb systems are too much for Newton's approach. There are too many moving parts. On top of the inevitable unpredictability of dumb systems, other complex systems aren't dumb. They adapt and evolve. Complexity scientists seek insights into how such systems work. They've had more success than Newton and his pals.

Complex adaptive systems evolve, and new behaviors emerge.

The poster child for complexity theory is the *complex adaptive system.*[4] Examples of such systems include *Cities* and *Hives* and *Species*, where the system is somehow greater than the sum of its parts. The system is composed of individual *Critters* (agents) just doing their thing. Somehow, something new *emerges*. Critters adapt but do not evolve. Systems *do* evolve and we can assume they're complex, so *evolutionary systems* might be a better definition. *Agent-based* systems is another relevant catchphrase of complexity science. The agents can be ants or people or whole tribes within "super" tribes. The worldwide, networked *Market*[5] is an evolving system of corporations, which are themselves evolving systems with agents (tribal *Members*) called employees. *Corporations* as a form of organization (tribe) emerged with the Age of Plenty. Emergence is a big deal in complexity science. It's rarer than everyday evolution, which tends to be slow but sure. Emergent events/behaviors *pop* onto the scene. The history of the universe is full of

4 Adaptive isn't the best adjective. Evolving is better!

5 The *Market* is the largest thing humanity has built.

emergence, as detailed later. The focus here is emergent behaviors within and between human tribes.

Adaption/evolution requires a memory.

Systems can evolve if they have a memory. Species use DNA to remember how to build a successful critter, where we define success as surviving long enough to produce viable replacements. Tribes use *culture* to survive and prosper. Both tribes and species *evolve*. Both demonstrate the phenomenon of *emergence*, where something new comes out of nowhere. Newton and his followers could not explain that, either.

Complexity tinted glasses

The mindset of complexity theorists is considerably different from Newton and closer to Aristotle. Perhaps it is worth a new alt.age.science in the context of an emerging way of thinking about how the universe works. It starts with the assumption that there is a *tendency* toward complexity written into the fabric of the universe: "If things can get more interesting, they will." Hopefully, this mindset will help readers improve their own models of how the world works.

My Model

Brainy critters have a model of the world in their heads.

Everybody has a *model* in their heads of how (they think) the world works. Anything with a brain does. The model translates incoming photons and sound waves into a "picture" of the animal's surrounding environment. The *Mind*, a mental model made by "smart" critters is one of the premier instances of emergence in the history of life. Worms get by without a mind, but they're not very interesting.

My background

My model of the world is more formal than most. My field is operations research, which is mostly about making models (of processes). These models can be simple enough to fit on the back of an envelope or complex computer simulations. I'll *pretend* to build a simulation of how the world works called LifeSim. Consider it a learning tool. In pseudo-Java, my language of choice, *objects* are nouns, *methods* are verbs, and *attributes* are adjectives describing the characteristics of the objects. It has *classes* of objects and individual *instances* thereof. IBM is an instance of class Corporation, which is a "child" (sub-class) of Tribe. Several major classes in LifeSim have been mentioned already: Tribe/Member, Critter, City, Corporation. These are in italics the first time mentioned and capitalized later if I want to make a point. I capitalize a lot.

My model comes from four Muses.

My model is based on the works of my four Muses: William Shakespeare, Isaac Newton, Charles Darwin, and Douglas Adams. Shakespeare set the stage for Newton and his followers to define how the universe worked...before Einstein confused everybody.

Four Muses Model

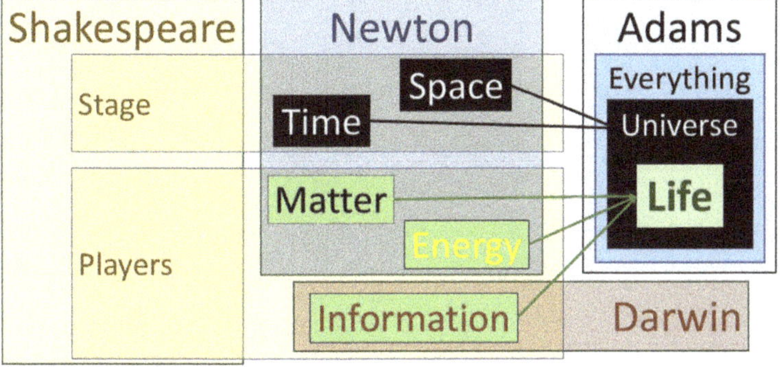

Elements of the Universe

The universe is simpler if it's made of fixed Time and Space.[6] Newton couldn't explain life, though. Life is made of Matter and driven by Energy, but until we recognized the role of Information (in DNA), we didn't have the answer. We credit Darwin for that. Douglas Adams, of course, had an answer for everything.

Two forms of life

In my model, there are two forms of life, *Critters* and *Groups (of critters)*. Critters includes all the plants, animals, fungi, and micro-life of Earth. Critters are composed of Matter and constructed according to the Information in DNA. Critters run on Energy. (Think calories!) Energy, Matter, and Information are the three ingredients in the recipe for Life. It's hard to pinpoint any Energy used by Groups of critters, whether *Mob* or Species. Also, groups have no more Matter than their members. Therefore, we assume groups are made purely of Information (genetic or learned). Groups, in some ways, *react* like living things but are not technically alive, just a *form* of life. Every herd or flock is a mob of critters. If the mob develops a culture, it graduates to tribe. You can't understand life on Earth

---

6 The "Elements of the Universe" get special treatment: Small Caps throughout

by just studying its critters. You need a model that accounts for group behaviors.

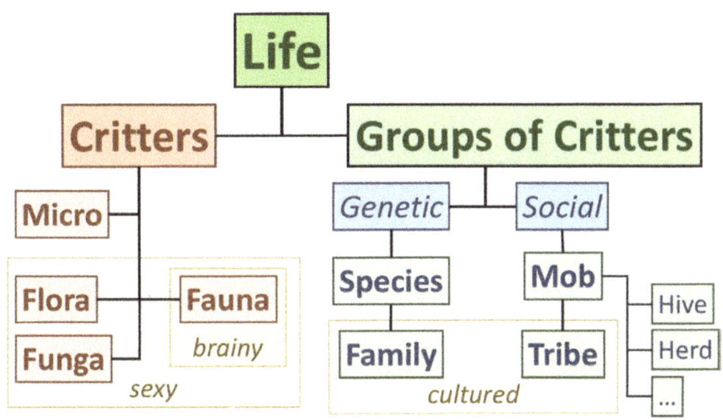

Tree of Life

Karl Linnaeus, Sage

The Swedish naturalist who drew the first Tree of Life ranks just below the four Muses. Of his original branches of Vegetable, Animal, and Mineral, the latter was soon truncated.[7] Later, RNA analysis gave us the domains of Archaea, Bacteria, and Eukaryote. Here, these are all on one branch: all the animals, vegetables, fungi, and micro-life are the *critters* of Earth. The only other branch of life is the *groups* of

[7] but at least we got a party game out of it.

critters on Earth. The focus here is on the human *tribes* of Earth. We are social critters. Tribes are how we socialize. Mobs are how we riot.

Models within models

My model has several detachable sections. There are mini models in multiple dimensions in both cartesian and polar coordinates. There are things to measure and things to categorize. One of my favorite methods of categorization is the Five-Bin Model. This lumps people (or whole tribes) into five categories/bins. The center category is *Normal*,[8] no matter what characteristic is being measured.

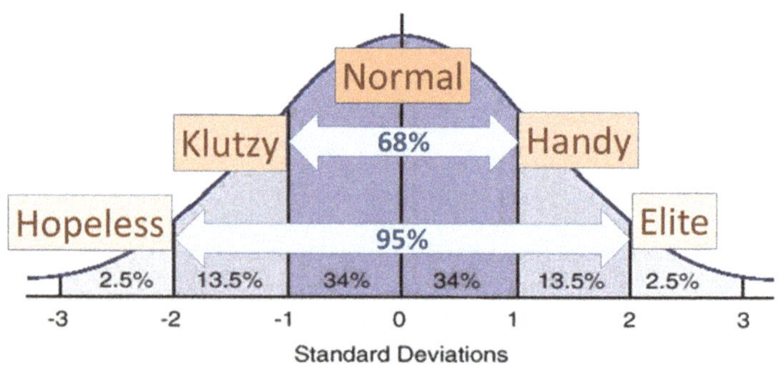

Normal Distribution of Competence

8 We also capitalize Bin labels and italicized them the first time mentioned.

The end bins are extreme, in opposite ways. The categories in between normal and extreme aren't quite normal (as measured by the normies!) but aren't crazy, either. This chart shows a Five-Bin model of general competence. Given *any* task, most of us (68%) perform normally. 2.5% are so much better at it (whatever *it* is) that they are Elite, i.e., crazy good. At the other end are the totally inept. The other two ("oddball") categories are sometimes the most descriptive. The short name for this chart is the Klutz axis.

Critical tribal characteristics

Five-Bin models are useful in defining several critical characteristics of tribes. The Control Stack measures the "tightness" a tribe has over its members. This is equivalent to the standard left/right axis, just turned vertical because verticality has better idioms and fits on a slide. The Xeno Axis rates a culture's attitude toward outsiders. (Both Great Memes triggered *major* changes in "normal" foreign relations.) The third is the Change Axis, which measures a society's *adaptability* to the changes the world keeps throwing at them. There is also a Risk Axis, in which rich cultures are recently catching "Safety Culture" memes. These four *measures of merit* describe critical characteristics of a tribe that allow it to survive and prosper.

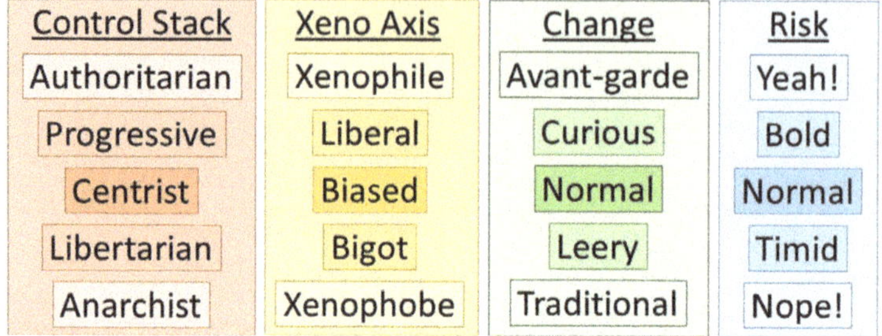

Four Measures of Tribal Attitudes

Lessons

This book presents my model of how the universe works. You might use some of its ideas to improve your own model. A familiarity with the basic concepts of *complexity science* can help you appreciate dynamic, evolving systems, specifically:

- You have several tribes and limited loyalty, time, and energy to give them.
- Tribes that lose their original purpose have been corrupted. You should leave.

- You are responsible for your behavior, so follow good memes.

  Don't pretend you don't know good behavior from bad!

- A bit of chaos is a good thing.

- There are still Barbarians about.

And Everything Else

This book presents my *model* of Life, the Universe, and Everything. You have a model in your own head of how the world works. Mine includes *complexity theory*. Yours probably does not but could benefit from a familiarity with the subject. Complexity theory is the most recent *paradigm shift* in scholarship. Thomas Kuhn[9] compared such new pathways of thought to taking off one's rose-colored glasses. That happened with Einstein and Heisenberg. They changed everybody's models of how the universe worked. Complexity theory can't hold a candle to those guys, but it's worth a listen.

My second goal is to impart an appreciation of *models*. They are all around us. Beware.

[9] Sage and author of *The Structure of Scientific Revolutions*, 1962

Models and Maps

Amateur model-making

You are a model user. You use models every day, with every word. Every story you create is a model of past events. Its accuracy is good enough for a court of law. Mathematicians use models more accurate (truthier) than yours, but only for highly specialized events. You can add to the truthiness of your story with numbers. Your model of the world has more than math. You can read or draw a map, which is something no other animal can do. You make and use models more than you think, but you don't get paid for it. (I did.)

Getting paid for a successful model

A job in operations research involves a disciplined effort at model-making. The customer has a problem and a question for the analyst to answer. The modeler needs to know enough about the customer's operations to create a model and answer the question. It may happen that it was the wrong question. That's when you know it was worth the effort to build that model.

Scale and Resolution

Simplification

The key to a good model is proper simplification. Good models are a subset of reality at an appropriate level of detail to transmit the INFORMATION effectively. If your question is about automobile travel, you need the level of detail provided by a gas station map. In tactical combat, you're going to need a better map. "Better", in this case, is defined as more detail or *higher resolution*. It is also associated with large scale maps. Small scale maps have fewer details and are of low resolution. (It's easy to go dyslexic on this.) The LifeSim model described below is of *low resolution* and low detail. For instance, we sum up all of man's ability to make and use tools in one capability/function/sub-routine[10] called Human.Reshape(MATTER). A high-resolution simulation would have exquisitely detailed *methods* like Human.Carve(Soap). (*Human* is a subclass of Warm/Brainiac/Fauna/Critter. You are an *instance* of that class! Reshape() is a method unique to humans.) We can add more detailed activities as needed. For instance, we added Human.Smelt(Metal) when describing the history of MATTER in the universe. Nature separates metal from

[10] Called a *method* by the developers of Java; one of their poorer word choices.

rock on a planetary scale. Humans do it in smaller batches. That method triggered the Bronze and Iron Ages, which rank among the top ten ages of most historians' *alt.ages* lists. In the jargon of complexity scientists, smelting was a major *emergence*.

The King's cartographer

"More Detail!" the king demanded of his cartographer, who went back to work...repeat twice for the standard-length anecdote...until the map was the size of the kingdom. To see the far corners of his realm, the king still needed a horse! This king just didn't grok maps. The essence of mapping is that we lose irrelevant detail in favor of a meaningful subset of the information. Seek the core, Grasshopper.

Word models

The first exclusively human models were words. The first word may have been a *Name*, a distinguishable noise (proper noun) that stood for a particular Member of the Band.[11] Humans then invented verb noises and more generalized noises for *classes* of objects (common nouns). These noises convey to your listener your model of what the hell just

[11] Later, you'll meet band member Og, the hunter who died doing that.

happened. Explaining what you think happened needs to be done at the proper level of detail unless you're long-winded. A *Story*[12] should be of an appropriate length to convey the relevant information rapidly and unambiguously.

The stories in your head

An animal mind interprets incoming sights and sounds (INFORMATION) and builds a model of its critter's immediate environment. Your *Model* handles the real-time aspect of INFORMATION, the present. The past is the realm of *Memory*. Your brain uses its memory to record your stories. Experience is the best teacher. Your experiences modify your model. You gain wisdom from your experiences unless your model is broken. We can blame all sorts of insanity on broken mental models. This is the root of the phrase, "He's out of his mind!" Parts of the model might break, for instance, the risk management algorithm for a criminal that thinks he can get away with it. But evil acts are not necessarily caused by a broken model. Some folks just prefer bad memes.

---

12 A *Story* is a sub-class of *Lore,* which stores tribal INFORMATION. Memes are a subclass of Lore, too.

Model (adjective) behavior

Beyond your instincts, you choose how to behave based on your own experiences and, if you're tribal, the wisdom of others. Memes are the composite of input from various tribal elders, as integrated into your model. Memes suggest behaviors, but the individual makes the choice. An individual that consistently chooses good memes, as judged in terms of tribal success, is a model citizen. For every positive meme that helps the tribe, there is a counter-meme consistently preferred by individuals known collectively as "bad eggs." They are not known for helping their tribes survive and prosper. In the context of commitment to the tribe, we can rate members on their willingness to submit to the tribe's goals rather than pursuing their own. There are, as usual, crazies at both ends of the spectrum. Rebels disobey the rules most often, demonstrating little will to submit to that tribe's social contract. Yes-men obey fanatically. Most of us (assume 68% in a Five-Bin model) are Normal or only a bit Naughty or Nice.

Interactions

There are two kinds of people in the world, you and everybody else. Unless you are a hermit, you survive and prosper by *interacting* with everybody else. There are four basic types of human interactions: one-to-one, one-to-many, many-to-one, and many-to-many. The last is the province of tribes. A speech is one-to-many. A good speech gets many-to-one applause. When you talk to a representative of the tribe, it seems one-on-one, but there's a whole tribe in the background. When one is sent to jail, it's because the many objected (strenuously) to the one's behavior. *Interactions* happened long before humans or even Life. They go all the way back to electrons and photons. If a thing doesn't interact with other things, it isn't very interesting.

Game Theory (Operations Research 101)

Interactions have winners and losers. In game theory, we call having exactly one winner and one loser a *zero-sum game*. In other interactions, both sides lose. War is the classic example of a *negative-sum game*, but any sort of conflict will do. In a prize fight, there is a clear winner and loser, but both fighters still get hurt. (This doesn't include the fans, who are the real winners.) As a fighter, you win some and lose some, so it's a zero-sum game in the long run. If there isn't a clear winner, like in many wars, both tribes just get hurt. Only with consistent victory does war look encouraging, but that's why empires are still a thing. The third sort of game is the *positive-sum game* where both sides win. The premier example is *trade*, but any sort of cooperation will do. If I have two rifles and you have two hunting dogs, we both benefit from swapping our second possessions. The big difference between the Age of Empire and the Age of Plenty is the games we play. Humanity has seen a long-term trend toward prosperity as knowledge has accumulated over the ages. Wars hid that progress but also caused chaos, which actually encourages progress! Nearby non-participants could benefit from that. The real winners, again, were outside the ropes, the onlookers to war.

The model faked here

Pseudo-code for a pseudo simulation

LifeSim is my model of Life, the Universe, and Everything, without the Universe or Everything. It is in pseudo-code status, nowhere near beta. Written in an *object-oriented* computer language like Java, the code for LifeSim would look like that shown in italics below. Object-oriented code focuses on the *objects* (nouns) in the system and how they interact (verb) with each other. The focus here is on Life, abbreviated *LivingThing*.

Program structure

Every object-oriented program has a main() method, which is a container for the class *declarations* and the *action* code, where the simulation really happens. The action can't start until objects in the sim and their capabilities are declared. The LivingThing object class comes first. Later come the declarations of its children, Critters and Groups. The action code hasn't been written yet (and we'll need a contract).

Why everyone needs to learn code

LifeSim code is a disciplined effort to reduce the description of Life on Earth to its minimal relevant elements. That's the essence of a good Story. Good code documents itself, said nobody who's ever tried it. The imaginary code below has comments after the double slash (//) just like real code, to describe the programmer's thoughts in too little space. The idea here is to reinforce some of the stuff you just read, which is why LifeSim is here at all, as a learning tool.

Style and Syntax

LivingThing is an *Object,* in standard Java syntax. Java objects are usually one capitalized word, but an unbroken string of capitalized words is legal. Objects are the *actors* in a simulation. They act by invoking a *method,* a verb followed by a pair of parentheses. The parentheses may be empty, which invokes the default action, such as Critter.Die(). A more detailed model might include a *parameter* (adverb or other specification) within the parentheses, such as Human.Die(Murder). This parameter isn't defined for any of humanity's parent classes, warm-blooded, brainy, animal critters. Critters in general don't commit murder, especially the plants. All the parent classes of humanity can use the default. If another species of critter is shown to be murderous we'll need another contract to expand LifeSim.

Top-Level LifeSim class declaration

We *declare* LivingThing below with five *methods* that define what it means to be alive. All living things, physical *Critters* or vaporous *Groups* (of critters) are children of Mother Nature and have one *attribute* that describes the "state of the system" (alive or not). Critters and groups of critters share these five critical *methods* (verbs): *Critters* React() to the environment by adapting, *Groups* react by evolving. Species Remember() chemically, through DNA. Critters and Tribes remember electrically through the Mind, a network of nerves with ions at the ends of their axons. Both critters and groups want to Survive() and Prosper(). They must Compete() to survive and prosper. Critters compete because ENERGY is scarce. They Prosper() if they get enough energy to replicate themselves. Groups of critters compete to increase their range (2-D SPACE), whereupon they Prosper().

```
class LivingThing extends Object {
//Attribute          Data Type    Comment
  Extant             Boolean      // 0 = dead/extinct
//Methods
  React( ) {sim code}             // Rocks don't react
  Remember( ) {... code}
  Survive( ) {...}                // You need this
  Compete( ) {...}                // You must do this
  Prosper( ) {...}  }             // You desire this
```

Classes and instances

LivingThing is a *class*, a template of the real thing. A class *constructor* creates "real" *instances* of objects of that class inside the simulation. (We spawn valid instances of "real" things much farther down in the code, with far more detail than "this is a living thing.") The only common *attribute* (adjective/descriptor/characteristic) of all living things is whether they are alive or not. When an instance of any living thing is "born," we assign it the Boolean value of 1 (True). When a critter dies (or a species goes extinct, or a mob disbands) we set the value of its Extant attribute to 0.

Parents on a string

The Class generates (*constructs*) "real" objects/instances as the simulation proceeds. Classes also have *child* (sub)classes, which we must define before the sim starts. The corporation class *inherits* its general characteristics from its *parents,* all the way up: LivingThing/Group/Mob/Tribe. The corporation class has a *constructor* method that spits out "real" corporations like IBM.[13] IBM is an *instance* of the class named Corporation founded in 1911 under another name.[14] They changed the value of its Name[15] attribute to "IBM" in 1924. It *inherited* its Extant attribute from the very top of the class hierarchy, the LivingThing class. IBM's Extant attribute is still set to "True."

---

13 Or as "real" as corporations *inside a computer simulation* ever get.

14 It was *instantiated* in 1911 if you want to sound like a geek.

15 We capitalize Names of LifeSim attributes, like Name, incidentally, in the text henceforth.

Inheritance

We created object-oriented languages for simulations because the real world is full of objects. Most are *physical* things like spoons or elevators. We call "things" that are less than fully physical *phenomena*. Rainbows are a combination of light and vapors but don't really exist without an observer.[16] Life itself is a phenomenon. Here everything is an *object*, even if it isn't a *thing* (having mass, made of MATTER, and occupying SPACE). Java organizes objects by Class on a hierarchical tree with the top object class on the tree being, unsurprisingly, an *Object*. This holds housekeeping and synchronization code that every object needs. In the code above, LivingThing *inherits* these capabilities and characteristics via the *extends* keyword. Inheritance is a big deal in Java. It saves a lot of repetitious code. As we get deeper into the details of life on Earth, we don't need to mention that every critter/animal/mammal/primate wants to survive. *Every* living thing wants to survive, and every real instance of life inherits the Survive() method from the top of the tree. All "child" classes inherit all the methods from all their "parent" classes. Child classes also inherit all their parent's *attributes*. These describe the *state* of the object. If

---

[16] As opposed to the fallen tree, which was loud even if you were not there.

you paint your car, you need to change the value of its Color attribute. Every instance of class car has a color. So does the class Car, though it doesn't need it for itself. A *class* is an idealized template for constructing real (simulated) objects like cars. Ideas are hard to paint.

Constructors

Most class templates have a *constructor* method that creates the real objects (keeping in mind that these are simulated "real" objects).[17] The constructor creates "real" *instances* of the class with the *new* keyword. For example, in the main()[18] program that charts the history of humans on Earth, a new *instance* of class Army (subclass of Tribe and Mob) emerged on the steppes of central Asia with the following code:

Army GoldenHorde = new Army()

We define the Mob, Tribe, and Army *classes* before the simulation clock starts. The GoldenHorde is a "run time" creation, a new *instance* born after the sim starts. This is different from being a new

[17] And that this is a simulated simulation. We'll cover recursion later.

[18] All Java programs start with a main() method.

child (class) of Army. The GoldenHorde was not a new *type* of army. They could use the standard Kill() and Take() methods inherited from the generic Army class. If the GoldenHorde had a unique technique of warfare, it might deserve a special parameter for its Kill() method. The Confederate navy might deserve a Kill(Submarine) parameter for that *emergent* capability. It takes a *major* emergence to justify a new Class in LifeSim. In this case, and with a decent contract, we would create a new class called *Navy,* child of Army[19].

A model of everything

LifeSim, if we actually built it, would model Life on Earth. A slightly more ambitious project would model the Universe and Everything. It would model the universal *tendencies* of complexity and entropy (creation and destruction) that drive the interactions that make the universe interesting. It would define classes for the elements of the universe: SPACE, TIME, MATTER, ENERGY, and INFORMATION, not that they, aside from living matter, are very active. TIME has only one method and used it just once, Time.Start() at the Big Bang.[20] SPACE had its

[19] like the Chinese Peoples' Army Navy

[20] Add Time.Warp() if you need Einstein in your model.

Dimension attribute set to 3. Space has one child class, the BlackHole. Energy only does one thing by itself. It disperses, due to the universal tendency toward entropy. Energy consists of physical bosons, but we are more interested in the phenomena that result from the *interactions* between Energy and Matter. Matter "owns" the capability to Interact() with energy or other matter. It would also need Matter.Attract() to simulate gravity, ChangeState() for its phases, and a Matter.Collapse() method to create a BlackHole. LifeSim is primarily concerned with living Matter. The methods defined in LifeSim simulate how living things like Critters and Groups of critters get things done.

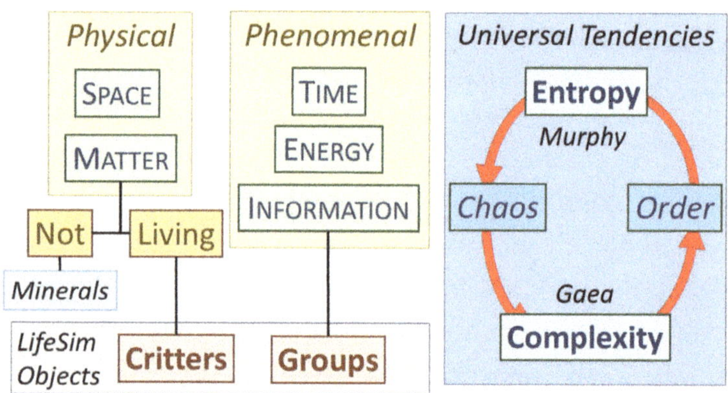

A Model of Everything

Complexity

The Minor Prophets of Complexity

Einstein and Heisenberg are the Saints of 20th century physics. It's harder (~impossible) to find as notable a representative for complexity theory. Ilya Prigogine received the first Nobel prize for complexity science. The Butterfly Effect, perhaps the best-known phenomenon of Chaos, comes from Edward Lorenz. James Gleick wrote the best book to popularize the subject. Norman Packard located the Edge of Chaos. We assign these four the title Agents of Chaos, with the rank of Minor Prophet.

The abandoned goal of complexity science

Originally, complexity scientists intended to "find order within the chaos" of complex systems. An uncomfortable number of systems were not behaving themselves, the weather for one. The hope was that we could "tame" these systems through better analysis. *Instead, complexity science "proved" that prediction was futile.* The main lesson we learned is that complex systems will forever go awry. Even with millions of sensors and awesome computer power, weather predictions will be wrong. Fortunately, despite punting on their initial objective, the analysts of chaos and complex systems have produced some very useful insights, some semi-famous.

Famous Complexities

The Butterfly Effect

The Butterfly Effect is perhaps the most well-known insight into how complex systems work. It concerns delicately balanced complex systems. A gentle tap, a puff of wind from a flapping butterfly in Texas perhaps, could tip the system into a wildly different mode. In this case, a tornado touches down somewhere unusual like Tokyo.[21] A less well-known phrase for this system behavior is "sensitive to initial conditions."

Simple systems can go chaotic.

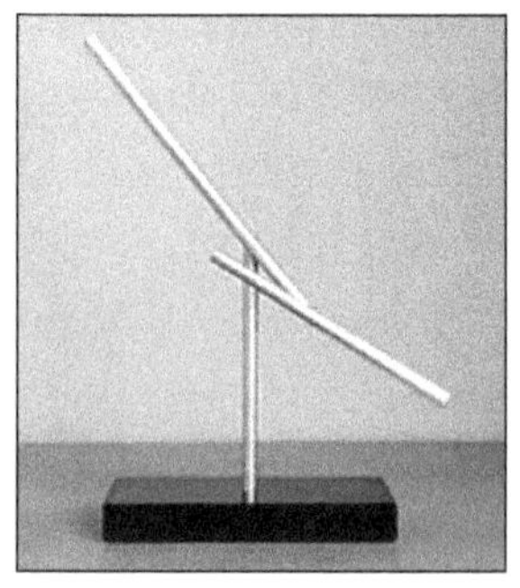

Double Pendulum

The double pendulum demonstrates a "chaotic" path with very simple components. One of the most solid insights that complexity theory provides is how easily such systems go chaotic.

[21] The location varies. This is not yet a "settled" science.

We have learned that it only takes three components if the interactions between the three is *non-linear*.

Three attractive bodies

The Three-Body-Problem was a well-known thorn in the side of Newtonian mechanics. The orbits of three gravitationally attracted objects would go "chaotic." Solving three simultaneous non-linear differential equations is tough enough. (In fact, there is no closed form solution.) On top of that, you obtained different orbits if you used more accurate values for *pi*. On a computer, you can reveal chaos if you use 16-bit instead of 64-bit math. Minor changes that "blow up" are characteristic of systems that are "sensitive to initial conditions."

Lorenz reads the weather

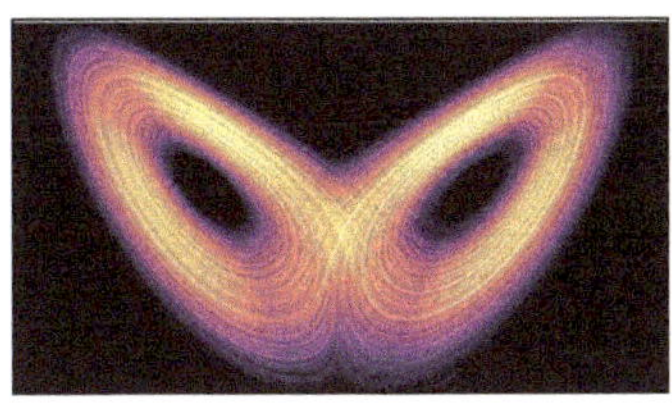

Lorenz Attractor

The same process occurred when Edward Lorenz restarted his weather simulation one morning, *using rounded off values* from yesterday's run. The wildly different results screamed "sensitive to initial conditions." Some systems have two preferred cycles and flopped between, "attracted" to one side or the other. (The parallel between this behavior and the flipping of Earth's magnetic poles every 50 million years has been noticed.) A simulation of a *Lorenz Attractor* is pictured here. The artwork keeps getting better for this phenomenon.

Complex system: Similarity at different scales

The Mandelbrot Set, another famous product of complexity science, has its digital artists as well. The Mandelbrot Set is viewed better live than with screen shots. It shows a common phenomenon in complex systems and fractal mathematics called *self-similarity*. You can see "ferns" in a closeup of the Mandelbrot Set. Zoom in ten more times and you'll see three or four more groups of ferns. The same pattern shows up at multiple scales. The same is true for tree/branch/limb/twig fractal art. The same rules apply at each scale, for instance, "branching at angle y at a distance x from the last junction." This kind of self-similarity is found in the vascular system from the aorta down to the tiniest capillaries and in bronchial branching as well. Artists use fractals to sculpt mountains from the top down. Video artists encode clouds and smoke using self-similarity. Slartibartfast used them on his Norwegian coastlines.[22]

Top-down self-similar organizations

Self-similarity is a good model for hierarchical structures, a common organizational pattern in large human tribes. The *Army* has a self-similar organizational shape. The guy at the top has ten guys who report to him, each of whom have ten guys that report to them, each of whom... Any hierarchical organization will have structures at each echelon that look much alike organizationally, even when they have different purposes. A *Country* generally has two or three layers below federal. Regional and local authorities (state and county in the US) cover every square inch of the Homeland except for embassies. *City* and native authorities lay over those. These spread the load of governance and justice. They are self-similar in one important way: They all have their own cops. Cops are the primary enforcers of the Social Contract. They bring to justice members who do things the tribe doesn't want them to do. Cops carry the tribe's big Stick, even for

[22] ref: @HitchhikersGuide

corporate tribes like the phone cops.[23] They don't get lethal sticks, but they can detain you on their tribal property.

Kardashev, Galactic Prophet

The scales at which humans operate has increased over the millennia. The size of our largest Tribes has grown. The next step may be a global civilization. Until we go interstellar, it will be the last expression of self-similar growth. The Scales of Man chart borrows from Nicolai Kardashev who

Scales of Man

Source	f()	**Tribe**	Kardashev Layer
Mammal		**Family**	I
Primate	Family +=	**Troop/Band**	II
Human	Band +=	**People**	III
Barbarian	People >=	**Empire**	IV
Trust	People +=	**Civilization**	IV
Borg	*Species*	**Humanity**	V
Meme			

Layers of Human Tribalhood

[23] ref: @WKRP

developed a scale for galactic civilizations. This version of the Kardashev scale has layers of human social structures. The family is the smallest Tribe, at a minimum just Mom and one cub. Primates socialize in troop-sized Mobs, graduating to Band if they develop a culture.[24] Humans, alone among primates, added a third Kardashev layer when we started talking. Thus emerged the people-sized Tribes, separated by language. The Barbarian meme inspired *Empires*, which are larger than any single People. So are *Civilizations*, which are a rather more voluntary association of peoples. A fifth level of human tribe involving the whole species will require a meme of similar impact to the Barbarian and Trust memes.

The Edge of Chaos

With respect to tribal evolution, one highly relevant concept from complexity science is the Edge of Chaos. Norman Packard coined this term in the late 1980s. It ties the rate of evolution of a complex system to the *stress* on that system. An older expression is, "Necessity is the mother of invention." Another relevant adage is, "Whatever doesn't kill you makes you stronger."

---

[24] Band is the second oldest Tribe, after Family

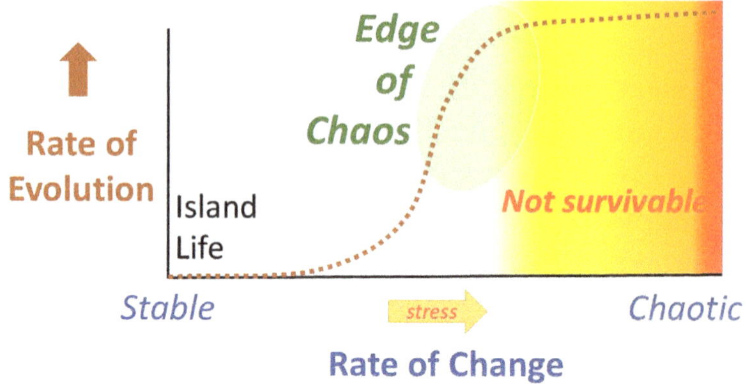

Sweet Spot for Evolution

Island life

Evolution slows to a crawl if there is no need to change. This happens on islands, which are seldom troubled by new species wandering in. But island species might pay the bill when new species *eventually* arrive. Life evolved on Guam without predatory snakes. One pregnant Philippine brown snake doomed 90% of Guam's native bird species. That might have been an airplane stowaway. Boats did more damage before airplanes emerged. Even rafts work, considering the fate of the largest native Australian lizards. The first humans to reach the new land learned that the dominant and tasty cold-blooded reptiles of Australia were not morning people.

Practice makes you flexible.

Stable conditions turn chaotic as the rate of change increases. The need to adapt increases. This favors *agile* species over specialists. It's like anything else in life, the more you practice, the better you get at it. Island critters don't get to practice their agility. They don't Survive() well when there is a sudden flurry of things to dodge. A species that inhabits a more dynamic environment gets a steady stream of tests. This keeps them on their toes. The same is true for tribes, especially corporations, which inhabit the worldwide Market, the most dynamic and stressful tribal system created by man.

Stress-free zones, the slow lane of evolution

There are other forms of stress on the system. The least stress from daily, seasonal, or millennial changes comes from living underground. The only significant[25] life down below is microbial, living a low-energy, slow existence with no need to change

[25] By some estimates, half of Earth's total biomass

in the foreseeable future. It's a safe bet they aren't going to evolve much compared to us sunshine eaters. Surface dwelling critters also have a latitude factor. Away from the equator, the stress of freezing occasionally or for several months matters as much to the flora and fungal subclasses of critter as it does to animals. They get tested every year.

Energy-rich lands see more action.

For mobile critters, the *value* of land changes with its productivity. Bountiful lands (and waters) attract the most attention. They support a wider variety of life. Wandering mobs of critters visit them more often. *Change* happens faster in productive lands. Barbarians invade farmlands more often than deserts. Barbarians are an outstanding source of stress if you wish your culture to evolve at a rapid rate, though barbarians and their Empires[26] can also create unsurvivable levels of stress. Many societies inhabiting good agricultural land went extinct in the Age of Empire. The surviving remnants of such societies would often prefer absorption into the culture of the winners than banishment to the food-scarce hinterlands. Societies that lose *leak*.

[26] Subclass of Country

Population density stress

A high population density is a good source of chaos and promotes a more rapid rate of evolution. Agriculture allowed more people per square mile, which triggered a change of priorities in tribal loyalties. When the first agricultural communities emerged (in Hyperborea 10,000 years ago), the people-sized Kardashev layer became more important. (The local Band was the primary tribal unit in the Stone Age.) The People, as an organized unit, became more relevant (and bonded more tightly) during droughts and other natural forms of stress. Barbarians represent a repetitive stress, which encourages a people-sized response. The Stone Age war chief is a temp position. The war chief segues to King when barbarians appear regularly.

High stress in the city

Cities achieve a much higher population density than farms or herding lands.[27] City dwellers have more encounters with strangers every day. Cities needed to develop successful memes to handle this, or they would have died. It's called being civilized. Higher population density also means that people of

---

[27] Herding is the other major behavior for obtaining Energy (food). Fishing is a form of hunting.

talent are not too far away. Cities increase the rate of change by maximizing the number and quality of human interactions. Cities make it easier for people of talent to get together, where they can make and trade things of value. All sorts of societal changes evolve faster in cities. Cities are on the cutting edge. On the Sweet Spot of Evolution chart, cities are at the upper right of the Edge of Chaos.

How do you feel about the pace of change?

Members of the Avant-Garde live in the city. People who prefer a slower pace of life move to the countryside, if they can. Below is a Five-Bin model of a "normal" population's preference for

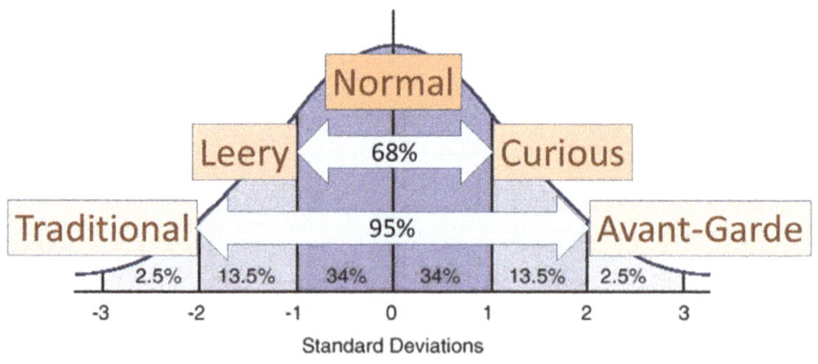

Change it Up? No...Yes

slow or rapid change. We can expect 68% of the population to have no strong opinion on the subject. 27% do have strong opinions, and the normies think them a bit odd, either too curious or too cautious. 5% of the population is quite nuts on the subject, either rejecting anything new-fangled or willing to try any new fad. Traditionalists want stability. The Avante-Garde favor chaos.

Traditional tribes missed a lot of memes.

City dwellers tend to prefer the right-hand side of this graph. In *Future Shock,* Alvin Toffler assumed that the modern world is changing faster and faster, perhaps too fast to remain sane.[28] Humans have different preferences for a "comfortable" rate of societal change. Pastoral tribes tend to the left. They are leery of change in part because they don't practice change. They don't get as many visitors, so they aren't exposed to new ideas. New ideas come from others more often than they are self-generated. At the extreme are tribes that reject *all* human interaction. The Uncontacted tribes haven't changed for thousands of years, so they are more than a wee bit Traditional.

[28] i.e., unsurvivable

The Newest Science

The history of science deserves its own *alt.ages*. We might name the ages after Aristotle and Bacon or other luminaries. Or we might label the ages by approach, where in the first age scientists just observed things and made mental models of them. With Bacon's meme, we started to *measure* things and improved our models. Then we reached the limit of measurement (and certainty) with the models of Einstein, Heisenberg, and Goeddel. We are now trying to compensate for the loss of certainty and knowability with complexity theory. In *alt.age.science,* we might define the Age of Observation, The Age of Measurement, and the Age of Compensation. Thomas Kuhn would call each a major paradigm shift.

The Age of Observation

Humans were observing the universe and making models of its components before the Sumerians invented calendars. The Greeks added geometry to explain the planets (poorly). Einstein was basically a geometer, not a measurement guy. Carolus Linnaeus observed life and modeled it after a tree. He didn't measure much either, though he and Einstein were born well into the Age of Measurement. In their approaches, they were more like Aristotle. Old memes die hard. There are still barbarians around, for instance.

The Age of Measurement

Newton's model, as it evolved since Bacon, represented the consensus view of how the universe worked until 1905. It represented the Truth (whatever that means) or as close as we could get to truth outside pure mathematics or logic. Measurement relies on numbers, which are as true as it gets. Still, measure twice, cut once. Measurement had its limits even without Heisenberg.

The Meme that died

For a quick example of how a meme can affect a society, consider the Clockwork Universe meme. This was the idea that the universe was as predictable as a clock, though a billiards table might provide a better analogy. If we could measure the speed and direction of each ball perfectly, and model friction perfectly, we would know where all the balls would come to rest. A "sufficiently advanced intellect" could track every atom and predict the fate of the universe. Pierre LaPlace, the spokesman for the meme and prominent Deist, had God in mind for the job of noting every sparrow's fall.

Classic Newton

The Clockwork Universe meme is classically Newtonian. Newton represents all the scientists up to Maxwell, who in 1865 unified light and magnetism. That nailed down the last errant form of ENERGY. The classical model consists of MATTER, ENERGY, SPACE, and TIME. It has worked very well for engineers, who keep building better, cheaper, and more accurate stuff. Engineers know they will never achieve perfect measurement, but ever-increasing accuracy still means never-ending progress.

The Clockwork Universe was a confident meme.

Confidence in the prospect that "things would keep getting better" spread throughout Western society. The peak of this confident attitude may have been the Gay 90s. It began taking hits at the turn of the century. In 1900, Max Planck reformulated how light worked. This would lead to the quantum realm, within which Heisenberg put a limit on accuracy. This absolutely killed the Clockwork Universe idea. Engineers didn't care but society, in general, had a plank yanked from under them. We have always sought truth, and Science seemed the way to get at it. That hurt.

Relativity and Unknowability chip away

Einstein removed another plank in 1905, with society interpreting his work (badly) as "Everything is relative." Certainty took another drubbing. This further reduced the confidence that we were on the path to Truth. Religious certainty may have peaked as well. Even mathematical certainty fell when Goeddel proved that in any language, you can always make a pun. The list of things in which we had absolute confidence shrank again. How influential was the Clockwork Universe model on society? For a while, it worked quite well. It helped produce a society confident that we were on the path to truth. The loss of this confidence might account for much of the malaise in modern society.

The pieces/parts approach: Scientific Reductionism

The principle of scientific reductionism, reducing the system to its parts and micromanaging the study of those parts, works very well in tightly controlled conditions. Engineers use Newton's model to design more accurate and efficient machines. However, chaotic conditions are far from tightly controlled. Newton's model was known to come up short in turbulent conditions. On his death bed, Heisenberg reportedly said, "When I meet God, I am going to ask him two questions: Why relativity? And why turbulence? I really believe he will have an answer for the first question." Despite Heisenberg's uncertainties, engineers plowed ahead with an attempt to simulate the weather, a well-known turbulent system (remember Lorenz?). They didn't get far, but we got better computers out of the attempt. Weather simulations funded the first super-computers.

Getting butterflies over your predictions?

We came to realize that no matter how many sensors we installed, or how fast the computer, we'd never get the weather right. A butterfly flapping in Texas just might spawn tornados in Japan. "Sensitive to initial conditions" is a mainstay of complex system analysis. Predicting the future state of the system seems doomed. But what do we do now? One strategy is a retreat, all the way back to Aristotle! We just observe the system and try to model it. We needn't abandon all forms of measurement. We can still count things and rank them. We can categorize things like Sage Linnaeus[29] did for the vegetable and animal kingdoms. We can compensate for the loss of knowability by seeking robust solutions rather

[29] the 20 Questions guy

than optimal ones based on predictions. However, favoring robustness over optimization will be a major change in the memes for designing products and processes.

The Age of Compensation

The Age of Compensation is just beginning. The Clockwork Universe isn't dead yet. Control freaks won't give it up. It still works fine for engineers working on "trivial" design problems. Engineers don't need certainty, just "close enough." Only philosophers worry about this stuff, but philosophers help define the memes of the times. Their influence has cost religious tribes much of their impact already. Freethinkers often reject religious and other traditional memes within their habit of questioning everything. They are more comfortable with the loss of certainty than those with religious convictions. A central tenet of complexity science is that certainty, when dealing with non-trivial systems, is a pipe dream. This tenet doesn't play well with one of the original purposes of religion, which was to explain the unexplainable. Newtonian science promised to explain but failed. Complexity science doesn't explain either but might make you feel better about not knowing.

Complex Adaptive Systems

Complexity science has its fingers in several pies. The focus here is complex *adaptive* systems. The first complex adaptive systems analysts modeled were species, societies, hives, and cities.

Adaptive systems need a memory.

The study of complex *non-adaptive* systems began with weather. Weather doesn't adapt or evolve, really. It's pretty much the same as it was a billion years ago.[30] Evolution is a long-term form of adaptation, which requires a long-term memory. Weather systems have no memory at all. Mother Nature has developed two forms, *genetic* memory and *cultural* memory. Lore is the tribe's memory tool. (Lore includes stories, memes, and SOPs). Genes remember how to build successful critters and "own" that Information for Species.[31] *Ownership* of the data is a big deal in object-oriented programming, part of a data integrity principle called "data encapsulation." You can't just grab another object's data. You must ask nicely.

---

[30] The emergence of an O^2 atmosphere might be the last "evolutionary" change in Earth's weather system.

[31] The word "meme" comes from a geneticist, Sage Richard Dawkins

Complex system diversity

The definition of complex adaptive system has some wiggle room. One loose definition includes the human body, where all those separate cells and organs cooperate to produce the magic of human life. It would similarly include a single cell, with all its organelles, as a "complex adaptive system". Here we use the more limited *agent-based* definition. The system is composed of independent agents, as similar as ants in a colony, as opposed to the body's diverse kidneys and knuckles. Bodies, human or otherwise, are marvelous complex *integrated* systems. They adapt during their lives, but do not *evolve*. Tribes and species are complex *evolving* systems. The rules are different for mortal complex *integrated* systems (class Critter) and immortal complex *evolving* systems (class Species or class Tribe). Also, critters run on ENERGY. Evolving systems run on INFORMATION. That gives them an entirely different attitude.

Agent-based complex systems characteristics–in bullets!

- They "want" to Survive(). They don't die of old age like their individual agents. They have a self-repair system to replenish dead agents and thus can last generations.

- They "want" to grow, more generally Prosper().

- They evolve, exhibiting new behaviors that *emerge* due to stress on the system.

- The original system formed spontaneously as an emergent event.

  You can form (instantiate) a new corporation on purpose, but the emergence of the corporation *Class* as a legal construct was not a planned event.

- Agent-based systems can display scale invariance and self-similarity. The same patterns are evident at micro or macro scales.

Emergence

The most interesting aspect of complex adaptive systems is their ability to produce new and sometimes unique behaviors. Complexity scientists call this *emergence*. The biggest example of emergence is Life itself. Sex and intelligence rank second and third.[32] The oldest critters have only a sense of taste to recognize edible chemicals. Sensing pressure (and

[32] according to some guy on Science Channel

doing something about it) emerged later. Sensing the environment from afar had to wait for the emergence of multi-cellular life. Organs for detecting odors, pressure waves, and photons emerged, along with a brain to interpret them. Teeth and claws emerged early, feathers and intelligence more recently. Here, the focus is not on the evolution of physical parts, like hen's teeth, but on the emergence of *behaviors*. Life gets more complex as new capabilities emerge. Emergence is not unique to evolutionary systems, but "dumb" complex systems usually have just one good jump in them.[33] Evolving systems keep changing. Life comes at you fast.

The City as an Evolutionary System

The *City* emerged to defend against barbarians. Its agents are its citizens. They go about their citizen business independently. The result is greater than the sum of its parts, the *City*. Scholars often describe the growth of a city as organic. It is the accumulation of the actions of all those independent agents. Cities sprouted in arable regions as the Ag meme spread. Those on major trade routes flourished. They are still here as the empires built around them have come and gone. As an independent sub-class

---

[33] ref: Ron Weasley *@ChocolateFrog*

of Tribe, the city-state has seen better days. We once manned its walls, which is the sort of thing that builds tribal bonds. Soon, though, city residents transferred their loyalty from the city (or its prince?) to king or emperor. Divorced of its defense responsibility, the city now exists to handle internal affairs like parking fines. Externally, city rivalries are now restricted to non-lethal forms of conflict resolution. Certain cities are known as football thugs, which says something about the behavioral xeno-memes of those instances of the City tribe.

Dense packing requirement: Develop crowd memes.

The original reason for people to gather densely (in the city) was to defend themselves. The reason that cities remain important, in war or peace, is that the number of interactions per day increases in the city. The number of times per day you might meet a stranger rises significantly. Citizens developed *memes* to compensate for the powerful stranger-danger behavior that nature built into our genes. When we tone down our naturally aggressive "anti-They" behavior, we are acting civilized.

Diversity of opportunity

The number of ways to make a living beyond hunting and farming exploded in the city. The Division of Labor meme found its natural home there. Women had always gathered, men hunted, and the band might have had a guy named Flint. The first guys named Carter and Carpenter appeared in the city.[34] People succeed at creating complicated things when they combine specialized talents. The most successful people are those who can coordinate the actions of the most talented people. That's how you can become a king. The city is the place to find the most talented people (Elites), where there are many of them not too far away. *Talent* is a key element of the INFORMATION domain. How you encourage and allocate talent is critical to tribal success.

Keeping up with the neighbors

One statistic that captures urban success is the *pace of change*. Things happen faster in the city. If the neighboring People have a city, you cannot keep up without one. Both peoples are not just in an arms race. They are in a social development race. The competitive environment is not just dynamic; it is

[34] Smith was a barbarian.

changing at an accelerating pace. Cities are the key to keeping up with the Joneses.

Super Systems

The biggest complex adaptive system

Complex adaptive systems can range across scales from local to supersized. Human tribes scale from family to clan or nation and civilization. Life on Earth is an evolving supersystem, where the agents are whole species. This is the largest complex evolving system we know of. It encourages its species to adapt and survive with the law of the jungle writ large. Evolve or die.

The second biggest evolving system

Each corporation is an instance of class Tribe (of Kardashev level II), with a culture that preserves knowledge and suggests behaviors. It is immortal and has a social contract with its employees and meets all the other qualifications for tribalhood. The corporation exists within a worldwide system of trade (the Market) that is the biggest thing humanity has built (without meaning to. It just *emerged.*) The agents of this supersystem are the corporations and individuals that join up. They agree to a social contract that reads, "Keep your promises or you will be cast out."

Keeping promises

The free market requires an unmatched level of kept promises. No form of landholding Tribe (Country/Empire/Clan) has ever been totally honest. That's what diplomacy is for. Political parties, one of the newest sub-classes of class Tribe to emerge, can survive a remarkable string of unkept promises. Corporations that consistently break their promises will lose trust and not survive in a free market. Money is a promise. Early paper money had "Promissory Note" printed on it. It replaced "Gold Certificate" which was also a promise. The enduring value of gold is, again, just a promise: "I promise you can take this coin to market and buy whatever you want." Governments that break this promise get inflation. Governments can also betray trust if they bail out corporations that couldn't keep their promises.

Tribes as Complex Adaptive Systems

The second complex adaptive system studied extensively by complexity scientists was the human *society*, another way of saying "tribe." Human tribes have all the characteristics of complex adaptive systems bulleted above, plus a justice system for resolving conflicts between individuals.[35] Members agree to submit to tribal justice. Otherwise, anarchy reigns. Loss of members' confidence in the tribes. Arbitrate() function can lead to the death of the tribe.

Tribal goals

The operative goal for a tribe is to preserve, transmit, and refine the memes that make the tribe successful. These are within the Elder.Meme() method. Sub-classes of tribe have specific goals beyond Survive() and Prosper(). A new class of tribe wouldn't have *emerged* if that goal weren't needed, and its instances wouldn't have survived if they didn't succeed at achieving that goal. The oldest tribe, since Mammalia, is *Family* with its goal RaiseSurvivableYoung(). The earliest humanoids–not just (talky) humans–used Band.ObtainEnergy() to hunt together and Band.DefendTurf() because they (and we) are territorial critters. When we began to talk, we formed peoples based on language and a new People.DefendTurf() method became necessary. Barbarian behavior brought forth a new tribe and tribal goal, Army.Kill(). The other Great Meme (the Trust meme) birthed Corporation.AddValue().

---

35 Non-human tribes use Critter.Duel(), with a Snarl parameter for threat displays.

The most important tribe to emerge after those two might be the Bureau. It has evolved within modern nations (subclass of Country) to perform the DenyPermission() function, wherein some members of the tribe are dedicated to preventing any members of the tribe from doing things most of the members of the tribe have decided to disallow. The "bureaucracies" of kings or emperors focused on collecting taxes. The Country.Tax() method makes funds available to kingdoms, empires, and modern Nations. Clans, the last major turf-defense organization, defend a *territory*, not a country. Clans don't have taxes or bureaucratic tribes or the Rule of Law or democratic memes.

Evolutionary pace

As the two major examples of evolving systems on Earth, *Species* and *Tribes* share important characteristics. One area they differ is in how fast they evolve. Memes allow a faster response than genes. Genes are based on chemical interactions while memes are based on electricity. Nerves transmit information using ions across membranes. This is faster than DNA but slower than an electric charge can travel along a wire. We might, therefore, expect artificially intelligent computers to evolve faster than Tribes or Species. Yikes.

Complexity as a Meme

Assume predictions are futile.

Complexity theory *starts* with the attitude that there are things we will never know. One nagging problem of classical physics hinted at this. *Turbulent* flow was unpredictable then and will remain so forever. Complexity science says so. It helps to start with low expectations. Then we aren't disappointed when things slip from unknown to unknowable. We start with confidence that we *can't* predict the behavior of a complex system.

You can't handle the Truth

The lessons of complexity science might soothe the discomfort of being uncertain about the future. The Clockwork Universe gave us too much confidence in that regard. The recent erosion of religious conviction doesn't help our cultural confidence index either. A complexity meme might convince us we never had a handle on it anyway. As agents within a complex adaptive system, we just make it up as we go along. It's a bit anarchic. The control freaks hate that.

A religious interpretation

In my model, complexity is akin to a *force* that opposes chaos. Complexity is the creative *tendency* of the universe that battles the slow death that tends from entropy. These universal and opposing tendencies provide the friction to make things interesting. It's Order vs Chaos in one idiom and Good vs Evil or Light vs Dark in others. Here, complexity is Gaea, formerly goddess of Earth life. (She got a promotion.) She is married to Murphy, God of Chaos. Her sacred decree is, "If something interesting can happen, it will." Murphy was, in fact, among the first interesting things that happened. Together they create the eternal battle between Order and Chaos. They are quite a pair.

The Complexity of Systems

"Things" are either real, physical objects or phenomena. Anything made of Matter is real. Photons and such are real but don't do anything unless they interact with Matter. Space is real. Time is a phenomenon. Information is a phenomenon. Entropy is a phenomenon, characterized by consistent energetic interactions between material objects. Complexity is different because sometimes the interactions are *not* consistent. They can even be creative. *Systems* of interacting objects are the phenomenon that invokes evolution.

The Universe

This section describes my model of the universe. There have been a few dozen Great Events since the Big Bang. We investigate these from the perspectives of the five Elements of the Universe: Time and Space, filled with Energy and Matter in the unliving universe, plus Information. The number of significant events in the universe accelerated when the fifth element brought life to the universe. Each element has its own Great Events and *alt.age*. Covered below are the most important changes that have emerged in the immediate purview of the most basic elements of the universe.

Space and Time

My view of Space and Time has been outdated since Einstein combined them in 1905, but a model doesn't need to be perfect. It just needs enough detail to provide a clear and simple map. You may need a thick red line to show the freeway, but you don't need to know the number of lanes. The guy painting the lane lines does, so he needs a more accurate, higher resolution model. Good modelers tailor the resolution of the model to the needs of the customer. Since few of us travel at relativistic speeds, Einstein is out.

The Stage

The game starts.

The focus of this chapter is the Great Events of universal history...when something new and important *emerged* at the elemental level. Frankly, not much truly new has emerged in the elements of SPACE and TIME since the Big Bang. The universe began with calls to the methods Time.Start() and Space.Expand(). Also, at this point the Arrow of Time is set, Time.Arrow= "Forward."[36] This *attribute* was the first adjective in the universe. The second was Space.Dimensions=3. Some string theorists and other heretics claim it wasn't always three.

---

[36] We might not know the difference if Time ran the other way. See AntiWar.

Breaking symmetry

As the Universe emerged, it contained the purest of substances, perfectly symmetric in all respects. Early cosmologists (even before coining the term "Big Bang") called it the Primordial Atom,[37] later the universal ylem. It was the only thing in the universe for an instant. We, therefore, call it The Unity.[38] Its breakup was a major event in the early history of ENERGY. The Unity broke apart due to the universal tendency toward complexity, which works to make things more interesting. With only one thing in the universe, you can't do much except split it up and see if something interesting happens. (It worked!) The Unity split itself into four (or five) forms of ENERGY, some of which condensed into MATTER. TIME hasn't evolved since then, but a new kind of SPACE has emerged.

A new kind of space

Black holes form an edge in SPACE, an exit from the rest of the universe. This certainly counts as a new, *emergent* kind of space. A black hole model

---

37 Georges Lemaître, (1894-1966), Belgian physicist, cosmologist, and Catholic priest

38 From DC Comics. Spielberg called it the Allspark. Kubrick fans recognize its Purity of Essence.

would need a Time.Warp() method to accommodate a major side effect, if we resurrect Einstein. A black hole is a localized dent in the universe that leads to a very different, possibly "timeless," sort of space. But it is new, so it counts as an evolutionary emergence of one of the five basic components of the universe.

Space code

No new *kinds* of Time have emerged since the Big Bang. Black holes are irrelevant to our tribes, so "local" Space hasn't changed either. We assume any gamma ray damage to Earth severe enough to affect the evolution of human tribes is not SPACE's fault. Technically, that's an ENERGY issue, a graviton to photon conversion in the gamma spectrum. The Star.Die() method calls the Gravity.Suck() and Matter.Collapse() methods. An if-then-else statement considers the dying star's *Mass* attribute and changes its *Composition* attribute from Plasma to White (dwarf), Neutron (star), or BlackHole.

Local Regions

While TIME and SPACE have not evolved from their original forms, we now perceive different regions *within* each.

Life needs a past.

The emergence of life certainly counts as a major event in the universe. With respect to TIME, the universe was not using *any* information from the *Past* before life emerged.[39] In a lifeless universe, only the current state of the system and its ongoing processes matter. The primary process before life emerged was *entropy*. (It still is. Life has not made *that* much of a dent in universal processes.) The main drivers of entropy are Energy.Disperse() and Matter.Mix()[40]. ENERGY and MATTER can do these things without knowing history. Life needs to know what worked in the past. Life needs LivingThing.Remember().

Humans invent the future

For unliving material things in the universe, TIME consists only of an eternal *Present*. (Photons have less than that; time doesn't even *happen* for them.) Living critters are born from successful patterns of INFORMATION from the *Past*. In only one of those Critters (hint: it's us) has the concept of a *Future* emerged. When did humanity start? One criterion might be, "Which hominid first scheduled

[39] Except for quantum information. Don't care.

[40] Ease of mixing: Plasma > Gas > Liquid > Solid

something?"[41] Since then, we have developed a model of time with regions labeled past, present, and future. (That is a linear model. Some religions have a circular model of time, no doubt derived from the way days and seasons keep repeating themselves.) We have schedules and plans and promises to keep. We also *spend* time on tribal duties, keeping our tribal promises[42]. How much time you spend on your tribes says a lot about who you are.

(Assumption) Humans make things "better."

As the first critter to contemplate the future, we are the first to Plan(). Most of us make plans to make things better. Some just want to watch it burn, but that's rare. Even barbarians envision a future with more food and mead. We work to improve our tribes because that enhances our survival and prosperity. We teach our children well[43] so they will take care of us when we're 64. Humans are very interested in that region of TIME we call the future. We make plans, promises, and predictions to make the world better.

[41] or made a promise? *Not time-related*, "Which hominids first called each other by Name?"

[42] Or we spend Me Time on ourselves

[43] Source: Crosby, Stills, Nash, and Young

We will assume that everyone reading this wants to make the world a little better during their lives. You can make an impact that outlasts your physical self through your tribes, family first. You strengthen your family by giving your children better memes. You can help your corporate tribe with better SOPs, but they won't last as long. An artist bequeaths items unto all of humanity, a particularly tribeless donation. (Humanity is a species, not a tribe.) Altogether, things have gotten better, or at least more interesting, which is the norm for successful evolving systems.

Regions of Space

The most interesting spaces are those on the surface of planets. On any planet, gravity separates SPACE into up and down. Wet, rocky planets have boundaries at the shorelines that separate two very different living conditions. A model of undersea life would need three dimensions, but fish are not the customers here. The rest of us suffer the shackles of a primarily 2-D existence.

Up and down sides

The vertical dimension arises in a social context. The Control Stack is appropriately vertical in the phrases "top-down" and "bottom up." Top-down is the preferred method of social control for generals and dictators. Bottom up is the preferred direction of libertarians. Memes change from the bottom up "in nature," which ties in with other vertical phrases. Grass roots change comes voluntarily from a groundswell of support. Top-down change dictated from above is enforced by the threat of violence. Still, it's good to be the king.

Splitting physical 2-D SPACE

The shoreline is a natural 1-D boundary between incompatible regions of MATTER, wet or dry. A *border* is a mental boundary that separates compatible regions. Borders are created by critters that choose to obey them. Territorial borders are, therefore, a function of INFORMATION, which has consequences in the SPACE dimension.

Other natural boundaries

There is a natural boundary around each species: its range. In addition, boundaries *within* the range of a species mark the 2-D space "owned" by *territorial* critters. Non-social predators like cats and bears often mark their borders. This behavior emerged as an alternative to the basic Critter.Duel() method for settling border disputes. (So did threat displays, but much earlier.) Social predators like wolves often form "well ordered" territories. Satellite tracks of radio-tagged wolves in Slovakia show sharp borders from their Pack.Compete() activities. There are six named Herds[44] of caribou on Alaska's North Slope. They don't meet often. Prey mobs tend to mingle and merge rather than compete for territory like predators.

Human precision

Modern human tribes have had well-defined borders since the Age of Empire. Civilized folk live in well-mapped *Countries*.[45] These are the regions of SPACE most relevant to the territorial tribes of man. Tribes want to grow, and emperors spend considerable effort doing so. Kings will take what they can get. The basic expansion meme of empire is an offshoot of the barbarian meme and related to the Dominate() behavior of all social critters.[46] The expansionist tendencies of modern nations are less aggressive, though they have expanded into "unorganized" territories without compunction.

44 Pack and Herd are sub-classes of Mob.

45 Empires, Kingdoms, and Nations are *Countries* with firm borders. Clans and Stoners have *Territories*.

46 Individuals genetically range from Bully to Doormat on this axis.

The US expanded into Indian *territory* and didn't stop until they met a *country* border at Mexico or Canada. Civilized cultures might celebrate certain Stone Age tribal traditions but have not respected their territory.

Personal space

An individual's critter's "personal space" is as far as they can reach. Unwanted intrusions on this space are not acceptable. This is fighting territory, but there are instinctive behaviors and memes for avoiding that. For many critters, there is a small region of "Flee!" just outside their fighting space. Lion tamers use that.

Land "rights" in the Stone Age

The homeland has been divided into lots for legal purposes since the Ag meme. Before that, the most valuable 2D space was good hunting grounds, a tribal asset at the People and Band Kardashev levels. Individuals didn't own any specific piece of ground. The best sleeping spot in the cave might be considered valuable space, more for a family than an individual. Such a space has *value*, which can trigger the Compete() and Dominate() methods.

The Status ratings for certain families within that band may change.

Agricultural Age space

Farmers might work specific parcels their whole lives, but their ownership of that land has varied widely. Slaves, sharecroppers, and commune members get no land titles. Anyone below *Lord* would have zero chance of land ownership in many empires and kingdoms. Innkeepers may have obtained de facto property rights before farmers. The lord might *grant* land to individuals, which effectively became family assets. The family homestead is the default Ag age landform if the lord is far enough away.

Timely property rights

Property rights covered personal property long before personal land. When we started putting in the effort to make tools, the toolmaker owned those tools. Even in the Stick Age preceding the Stone Age, we respected each other's sticks. Artfully *reshaped* MATTER has value for its usefulness and for the time the artist put into it. TIME is a deep basis for personal property rights, whether land or portable property.

Possessives (elements of the environment)

Below are "things" one might own. They take no actions by themselves, so they get no methods.

```
class Thing extends Object {
//Attribute    Data Type      Comment
  Mass         Float          } // in kg
class Tool extends Thing      {// reshaped MATTER
  Creator      Human
  Owner        Human          }
class Homeland extends Area  {// 2-D SPACE
  Owner        Country        }// Defender
class Lot extends Area        {// Post Ag meme
  Owner        Tribe          // Corporation, church...
  Owner        Family         // Homestead
  Owner        Human          }// Tribeless
```

Land rights

Land has been partitioned into lots and owned since the Ag lords OK'd it. The family unit was often the recognized owner in the olden days. As custom ceded to law in the Age of Plenty, individuals and tribes could own land. The tribe that has squatted on that land claims Homeland ownership. Empires don't always listen to such claims.

Other Dimensions of Space

Cities as Zero-D network nodes

Cities at the intersections of trade routes are points (if the map is big enough). Of course, cities have physical *area*, which is the lower half of the population density equation. Much of the progress of humanity came from cramming a lot of people in a small space. Higher density promotes more interactions between the agents of the system and increases the pace of societal evolution. Cities are where it's at.

Lines (One dimensional spaces)

Certain 1-D Routes through Space have extra value to any critter brainy enough to chart a path. (Micro critters and worms don't follow Routes.) These special paths lie on the lines of least resistance to travel. Clever critters use them to save Energy. They save time, too, but generally only man considers that valuable. The land (2-D Space) nearest these paths has value to man and some ambush predators. Not many critters value Matter other than food and water, but witty critters value Information. That's why they're curious.

Networks

We model Routes in one dimension and the area within borders by two. In between are an infinite number of *fractal* dimensions. Trade routes connect nodes in a network with a fractal dimension between one and two. In a sparse network, each node connects only to its nearest neighbors. In a *dense* network, a node can connect to any other node. Air routes have a denser fractal dimension than rail routes. *Social* networks became fractally denser with mail, the telegraph, and the telephone. Each eliminated distance (1-D SPACE) from information transmission. They count as emergent events in INFORMATION history.

Non-contiguous 2-D spaces

There was a trend early in the Age of Plenty related to ships.[47] Empires and kings who wanted an upgrade to emperor were able to expand into areas far away from the homeland. Previous empires consisted of a central people (thugs) surrounded by their vassal lands. The Age of Sail allowed the bits-and-pieces empire. This variation of empire didn't

---

[47] To conquer Brittania, the Romans had boats. *Ships* are intercontinental.

last as long as the old-style contiguous empire, but it certainly had an impact on the tribes of the world.

Energy

An integrated concept of ENERGY was the last task in reducing the universe to the Newtonian Four. TIME, SPACE, and MATTER were already well-established elements of Newton's universe. Energy was "hidden" in several separate forms. Light and heat were two different things, as were sound, lightning, magnetism, momentum, and gravity. Newton's followers gradually reduced the number of different forms to one and called it ENERGY.

In the beginning, One Kind of Energy Becomes Four.

Four types of Energy emerged.

ENERGY of the purest essence was the first thing to come out of the Big Bang after TIME started so SPACE could expand and create room for anything to be in it. The purity of TheUnity broke into the four forces that drive energetic interactions to this day. Add the Dark Force if you wish to build your own model.[48]

[48] Copyright law is forgiving here.

For a brief span the four kinds of *gauge bosons* were the only things in the universe. We call this the Age of No Matter in *cosmic.alt.ages*. It lasted a gazillionth of a second, officially. Then the universe cooled and MATTER emerged. That was a big deal, to say the least. More on that below.

A quick history of the human concept of Energy

In 1852, Kelvin defined energy as "any kind of force across all branches of science." In 1865, Maxwell unified light and magnetism, reducing all known forms of energy to electro-magnetism and gravity. Later, physicists needed the strong and weak nuclear forces to explain radioactivity and to hold quarks together. These four forces drive energetic interactions between bits of matter. Dark energy, whatever that is, is not part of this model, as irrelevant as Einstein. The *electro-magnetic* force dominates life, mostly in the form of chemical energy.[49] *Gravity* is seldom a factor in the evolution of societies, though it is the ultimate source of nuclear energy. Nuclear energy (from the *strong* force) is becoming more important. If you ask an engineering firm to power the worldwide economic system for

49 Raw electromagnetic energy (lightning, by Zot) has impacted the lives of a few unfortunate critters.

10,000 years, and their answer isn't nuclear power, don't hire them. The *weak* force makes unstable isotopes stable, which generates dangerous but sometimes useful radiation. The weak force is a minor influence on human survival and prosperity unless the public's fear of it delays the transition to nuclear power.

Energy storage

ENERGY wants to disperse throughout SPACE. It is impossible to get most forms of energy to stay in one place. But you can *store* it if you can pile it up faster than it leaks out. The most important form of energy storage for critters is chemical energy. In photosynthesis, photonic energy is stored as chemical energy in hydrocarbons, abbreviated carbs. Your ability to store carbs allows you to eat once and stay warm all day. Without energy storage, everything would die at sundown. In LifeSim, we feed no ENERGY into the system at night. Critters manage to survive on their stored energy. *Groups* of critters don't use energy, so they don't care if the power is off.

The rickety stack

In a vertical, gravity-compliant model, the atoms in the carbs are "stacks" ready to collapse and drive the formation of ATP. Adenosine **tri**phosphate (A**T**P) is life's portable battery. It drives almost every process in every cell. On delivery, ATP is converted to adenosine **di**phosphate (A**D**P). It collapses from Tri- to Di-shaped, delivers its photon and then gets sent back to the recharging station. We can describe this cycle as the conversion of *one* high energy electron in the Tri-shaped configuration to a low energy electron in the Di-shape. That electron keeps us alive.

Class carb

As an object in LifeSim, class carb has "child" sub-classes fat and oil. Both store more energy than mere carbs. Fauna of sub-class Predator have an Eat(Fat) parameter specifically for their eating habits.[50] The sub-class Omnivore inherits the ability to digest meat from them. Inheritance is a core principle in Java. It saves having to write the same code multiple times. Here it saves one line of code in every Canine/Feline/etc. predator subclass declared hereafter.

---

50 Herbivores Eat() default carbs. Flora.Eat(Photons). Funga. Eat(Booze).

Energy stored as Matter

There is one significant form of energy storage older than life. It occurs during the death of a very large star. Moments after the nuclear fire goes out, the outer layers of the star rush toward the center. Gravity accelerates (sucks) the atoms inward. Some drop several million miles and can reach 1/3 light speed. Their nuclei collide with nuclei at the bottom of the gravity well and form heavier and heavier elements.[51] The gravitational energy is stored as nuclear forces, some of which can be recovered later, but only from Uranium or Thorium. You can try Plutonium, but you need to collect it soon after the supernova. It *leaks* through natural radioactive decay. Plutonium leaks Helium nuclei for millions of years. Uranium and Thorium take billions of years, so they're still easy to find.

Energy density

The gravitational energy stored as nuclear energy in Uranium and Thorium is denser than any form of electro-magnetic storage. It is on a par with the energy latent in hydrogen nuclei when combined in a (future) *fusion* power plant. Both fall far short

[51] The Weak force gets really busy!

of the maximal energy storage form, anti-matter. Anti-matter drove the USS Enterprise across the Federation to infinity and beyond. The emergence of anti-matter tech would easily qualify as a new Age in alt.age.energy.storage, if there was such a thing. The energy stored onboard the starship Enterprise must have come from nuclear or electro-magnetic forces unless they depended on something, you know, fictional. Star Fleet must make the anti-matter at home and ship it out. They could use hydrogen fusion or solar power if they built enough space stations. They might need to take apart Mercury for its metal. Solar power is, at its core, based on fusion energy, but we didn't start the fire, so it's all photons to us.

Energy density vs power density

Uranium (U) and Thorium (Th) are too valuable to waste in making anti-matter. As a compact source of energy, the fissionable metals are in third place after THeD (Tritium or ^{3}He or Deuterium, whatever your fusion generators run on.) Anti-matter is top dog, 100 times denser than either Th/U or THeD. The value of heavy element fission currently is in its simple implementation. A minimal engine can tease the energy out of Uranium or Thorium. If we can make fusion generators running on THeD as compact as nuclear power plants, we would not use Th or U at all. More likely, there will always be a niche for heavy metal fission power generation. This is a function of *power* density rather than energy density. The power density advantage of lightweight turbines over reciprocating engines is why they own the helicopter niche. Fission power will remain relevant until we no longer need large, fast, long-range submarines or moon outposts.

Practical Energy

Basic energetic needs

Critters consume electro-magnetic energy, in the form of somewhat unstable (rickety) chemicals, to keep their bodies running. They need more than this minimum to accomplish life's imperatives to grow and reproduce. For mobile critters, it takes energy to move, whether in pursuit of energy or avoiding other critters that are pursuing them for energy. Movement is a big budget item for mobile critters, whether they are animals or micro-critters. As for the other two of the four major branches of life in this model, the energy used for movement is minimal for plants. They can React(Track) the sun. "Growing in the direction of" is not movement. Most fungal critters expend no energy in movement. Slime molds have a specialized Move(Ooze) movement method, which the Micros invented. Some Micros have cilia to Move(Walk) and tails to Move(Swim). Only Fauna.Move(Fly). There are a few specialized modes like Mollusca.Move(Jet). Drifting with the current doesn't cost any energy, but coral "eggs" can travel quite far in this manner. Spider.Move(Balloon) doesn't cost any ENERGY but does cost MATTER, in the form of throwaway silk. This is quite unusual, though other critters lose MATTER for other reasons. Poisonous critters lose matter with every bite or sting.[52] Some critters squirt ink or bioluminescent chemicals to Survive(Distract). There is little need to include a separate budget for MATTER in human affairs, apart from the occasional spitball. The ENERGY and TIME budgets are the most relevant ways to determine the priorities of individual critters. Most Groups of critters don't have budgets, but Tribes have a budget for Talent (a child of INFORMATION).

Energy return on investment, EROI

Energy spent for the explicit purpose of obtaining more energy is critical to the Energy Return on Investment (EROI) equation. This is the energy returned for each unit of energy spent in finding/

[52] Every spell costs a pixie dust.

refining/shipping more energy. In the oil business, the EROI is about 30:1 these days. It was as high as 80:1 in the gusher days. Since then, we have needed to spend more and more energy to pump it up, so the EROI has dropped. It's now about the same for coal and natural gas, so we still extract all three. We must add heat to tar sands to extract the oil, which lowers the EROI. Call it 20:1, which is still better than wind or solar. Those are in the single digits and only survive in niche markets or with subsidies. We will eventually exploit tar sands as the oil runs out. There is a plan to heat Canadian tar sands with nuclear power, specifically molten salt reactors (MSR). This only works because the EROI of nuclear power is much higher, 75:1 for second-generation light water reactors. Much of the energy pumped into those systems is used enriching U-235, which would not be needed for Thorium-powered MSRs. (Enrichment is not needed for CANDU reactors either, but they spend energy upfront filtering huge amounts of water to obtain heavy water.) The EROI for Gen-IV MSRs could easily top 100. The pursuit of low EROI alternatives like wind and solar power is ludicrous in contrast to the potential of MSRs.

Soapbox time

In the sixties, Oak Ridge Laboratory developed two molten salt reactor prototypes. Fireball was the name of the first prototype. It was supposed to keep airplanes in the air continuously or until the crews went crazy. This would be bad because the planes would be carrying nuclear weapons. This was during the Cold War. The engineers at Oak Ridge sold the Pentagon on this project because they wanted to build an MSR. Fireball was a name chosen by engineers to sell to generals. Obviously, no PR people were involved. It turned out to be an appropriate name for the reactor that set a record for high temperature continuous operation. After five nervous days of approaching the deformation temperature for nickel-steel, they shut the Fireball down. No reactor has come close to that record since. (i.e., it scared the hell out of the engineers, which is hard to do.) The second prototype they built lasted five years. It could easily qualify as the most successful prototype ever, and not just among reactors.[53] It remains the only reactor to use different fuels, 233-U and 235-U. It was flexible in maintenance and experimentation. It was walk-away safe. The concept of liquid-fueled operations is far safer

53 The prototype Hula Hoop was ready to go from the outset.

than current pressurized, solid-fueled, water-cooled reactors, which can have a meltdown if the fuel separates from the coolant. Some isotopes then vaporize, which is how 131-Iodine gets airborne. The steam pressure inherent in current designs helps push the vapor out of the plant. An MSR is unpressurized. The fuel is dissolved in the coolant and can't separate. It might overheat, but there's a bucket for that. It's as close as we've gotten to "walk-away" safe. Add to that the potential to use Thorium as its fuel stock. There's more of that than Uranium on Earth (or in the asteroids). Thorium produces 90% less transuranic waste (aka *failed* fuel. Highly radioactive failed fuel is easily managed, so it's not really a problem, but reducing it is good PR.) *Successful* fuel atoms split into smaller atoms (fission fragments). Solid-fueled reactors produce these at the same rate so there are no savings there. In fact, liquid-fueled reactors have the advantage that valuable fission fragments can siphoned off only seconds after they split from their suicidal mother nucleus. This can happen while the reactor is still operating. A solid fueled reactor's fission products are only available by stopping the reactor and taking the waste out, every two years or so. All but the last few (potentially valuable) short-life isotopes are gone by then. Additionally, a Thorium based energy system would not need to enrich Uranium at all. Then we would know any nation enriching Uranium is doing it to produce bombs. But non-proliferation is another stupid reason for not embracing nuclear power. North Korea proved that. Waste disposal is a similarly vacuous argument against nuclear power, MSR or not. Radioactive waste from any reactor is easy to handle and has never harmed anyone. We trust engineers to keep planes in the sky. They can easily keep warm metal deep underground.

A short history of the EROI

The EROI statistic comes from marine biology, not the oil business. It helped explain shark behavior. Why did the shark decline to chase the small, fast fish? He must have figured the chase would be long and expensive, energy-wise. Also, the return on investment would be small, snack-like even. What was amazing is how the shark did those calculations without even a high-school education. It is apparently written in every shark's DNA to make choices that minimize energy use. The shark has an algorithm!

EROI doesn't matter when you run out.

The Age of Plenty started in a wood-fired, horse-driven economy. We grew extra grain to feed the horses and take advantage of their power. We spent a lot of calories chopping and hauling wood to feed our fires. We could not run the Age of Plenty on wood. Wood has only half the energy content of coal, for one thing, so an efficient wood mining operation might have an EROI of 15.0. Moreover, it can run out. Scholars have suggested an energy shortage was one of the reasons for Rome's fall. They couldn't even run one city on local wood. Rome's problem was *dimensional*. Trees are distributed in 2-D SPACE. Forests refuel themselves slowly, so we can tap them responsibly at a slow, steady rate. Coal is 3-D, where we model the vertical dimension in ages. We can tap the stored energy in coal at a far higher rate than wood. This allowed the Industrial Age, the latter and more energetic half of the Age of Plenty. (The first half of the Age of Plenty consisted of getting the rules right, a function of INFORMATION.)

Spending Energy

Energy spent not eating

When critters find enough energy for the day, they mostly rest. They need an incentive to do anything else. Fleeing for your life certainly qualifies. Curiosity can get a still fish to move, so that might apply to any critter with a brain. (Worms hunt, but "explore" only incidentally.) Higher animals spend part of their energy budget *playing*, which might use the same genes as curiosity. Burrowing animals spend energy altering their environment. Other than man and nest builders, few animals do this. Social animals spend time and energy bonding with their herd mates. Critters spend TIME and ENERGY on reproductive affairs on special occasions. Somehow, they don't need a calendar and can find the energy.

Matter

MATTER is the most obvious and "real" element of the Universe. It is the only element that occupies space, except SPACE itself. It has four normal phases, solid, liquid, gas, and plasma. Extreme gravity can form "degenerate matter" in white dwarfs and neutron stars. Plasma is the most common form of matter in the universe, stars being full of it (in case that trivia question pops up). There are specialized phases of matter like Bose-Einstein condensates. But if Einstein is irrelevant in this model, Bose barely deserves mention. (This is it.)

Valuable matter

Energetically "charged" matter

Matter is the element that likely first comes to mind if asked to name something valuable. Gold might come first – to anyone not hungry or thirsty. That is a uniquely human attitude. Most animals want only water and food. In this model, food is really ENERGY. We do not engulf any old MATTER (other than water) just to fill our bellies with mass quantities[54]. We seek energetically charged matter that we can digest. It is the energy (from formerly living matter) that is valuable, not its mass, though a full belly is deeply satisfying.

Kinds of matter: living and not

The MATTER of most interest to us is living or formerly living matter. We need to consider the mineral world, but don't often worry about air. Water is harder to obtain than air, so has *value*. Many types of inorganic matter are valuable to humans. Other animals want few minerals other than water. Cows lick salt and parrots swallow alkaline dirt for their tummy aches. Burrowing animals push dirt

---

54 ref: Fred Conehead @*SNL*

out of their way, which is the opposite of "wanting." Ejecting dirt costs a burrowing critter TIME and ENERGY, so its value is less than zero.

A brief history of MATTER

In the beginning

In the style of the Great Memes and the *alt.ages*, here are the Great Events in *alt.ages.cosmos*, beginning with one *highly* energetic event, and an emphasis on the evolution of MATTER. The first cosmological age was the Age of No Matter, in honor of matter's conspicuous absence at that point in universal history. The Universe was full of bosons, which don't interact with each other. Frankly, that's the only way you can fit a universe into a thimble. *Interactions*, up to and including human interactions, have ruled since then. Free quarks popped up an instant or two after the bosons, but they didn't remain free for long. The strong force glued them into protons and neutrons and a zoo of unstable-ons. Some were Anti, so there was this big war. We ended up being positive about it.[55]

[55] The consensus is that if we were made of anti-matter, we couldn't tell the difference.

Cosmic Age	Event	Elements
No Matter	Big Bang	Bosons (Photons)
M=E/c2	Condensation	Quarks, electrons
Strong	Anti-War	Protons (H^{+})
Cloudy	Fusion	He, Li (traces)
Clear	e^{-} capture	Atoms
Stellar	Fusion_II	Metals (> He)
Stardust	Gravity	Planets
Smelter	Man	Purity of Essence

After a few moments

The survivors of the Anti-War between matter and anti-matter were still hot enough – going fast enough – to Fuse() when they collided. The weak force turns a proton into a neutron, creating nuclear stickiness and forming Deuterium. Further fusion piled on, up to seven nucleons per nucleus.[56] A few minutes afterward, there are three atomic elements[57] in the universe, Hydrogen, Helium, and a trace of Lithium but nobody cares about the Lithium. Most of the Lithium will get "burned" in stars, later. Cosmologists found a discrepancy between

[56] There are no stable nuclei with eight nucleons (or five), so "piling on" stops. Nothing heavier than ^{7}Li.

[57] Seven nuclei: ^{1}H, ^{2}H (Deuterium), ^{3}H (Tritium), ^{3}He, ^{4}He, ^{6}Li, ^{7}Li.

predicted and measured primordial Lithium, which we will not address because we don't care.

Cool

The universe did little but expand and cool for about 300,000 years. A few stars might have ignited, but their light would have been absorbed by the free electrons and ions in the universal plasma. Then the universe cooled enough for the "naked" nuclei of H, He, and Li to capture the free electrons. The negatively charged electrons and positively charged nuclei joined to produce neutral *atoms*. Plasma became gas. Photons were then free to roam the universe, and the skies cleared. This was the origin of the Cosmic Background Radiation.

Fusion, round two

Not much changed in the realm of matter until stars formed and begin transmuting hydrogen into helium, then helium into carbon and so on. Chemistry was boring before then. The only available building blocks were H and Li. Helium doesn't do chemistry. This is not very interesting. Then stars fused hydrogen and helium into what astronomers call *metals*, i.e., nuclei heavier than helium. Metals are an important *emergence* in the history of MATTER.

However, the metals are locked in stellar plasma, and unable to be interesting, until their stars start dying. The little stars "puff out" elements up to (approximately) Calcium (atomic number 20) in *nebulae.* Stars big enough to produce Iron (atomic number 26) puff a bit harder. They go *supernova* and produce heavier elements, up to and beyond Uranium. The first (emergent) supernova in the universe must have been quite a surprise. Major emergences are like that, even in the lifeless universe.

Heavy matters

Note that nuclei with more than 83 protons (Bismuth) are unstable. Such nuclei decay to Bismuth (or Lead) unless they are Thorium or Uranium, which are still around. They were born in the "local" supernova that flattened our solar system into existence. (Mostly... a few U and Th atoms now on Earth might have come from older supernovae.) The ENERGY that went into making the U and Th atoms came from gravity as the supernova was collapsing. Much of that inward momentum was E=mc squared into MATTER in the form of heavier nuclei. The Th and U absorbed this energy and *stored it.* This is one of the few examples of energy storage happening anywhere in the universe. When we burn

Uranium in our reactors, we are releasing "clean" gravitational energy!

Aftermath of fusion

After a few supernovae and nebulae, the well scattered metals (and hydrogen) can form solids, gases, and, rarely, liquids. These can mix and combine to create the first "interesting" chemical compounds. Carbon, hydrogen, and oxygen can form simple organic molecules. The opportunities for complex combinations exploded with carbon. Gaea was pleased.

Non-living matter gets as interesting as it ever gets.

The number of compounds that can form in interstellar clouds is small. The number rises when gravity causes planets to form, and more if those planets are in the liquid zone for a decent solvent, like water. Liquid water as a solvent can transport atoms and compounds into range of each other, where they can self-assemble into complex substances like amino acids. Then, life as we know it can start producing its dazzling array of ever more interesting organic compounds.

A beneficial natural catastrophe

Gravity and liquidity allow the *natural* differentiation of MATTER on a large scale. Scholars of Earth history call this the Iron Catastrophe, which is a bit dramatic since no one was hurt. Iron and nickel sank to the center of the Earth and rock floated to the surface. There are a few other cases of natural *segregation* of metals, for instance, gold collecting in quartz deposits. Crystals naturally segregate themselves, which is about the most interesting thing that happens to unliving solid matter. Fluid matter gets more chances to interact with other matter and energy. Warm rocks are not very interesting until they melt. Energy added to fluids makes weather, which is always interesting, though perhaps not enough to justify space tourism.

Humans reshape matter

Gravity and heat forced the natural differentiation of liquid metal and rock in the Iron Catastrophe. Humans practice "unnatural" differentiation in a variety of smelting processes. Human smelters refine MATTER, an emergent behavior important enough to name the Bronze and Iron ages for the smelters' products. Refine(Metal) is a human-only method, a specialized method under the broader Reshape(Matter), which covers all types of toolmaking and tool use. Other animals (for example, nest builders) reshape local materials for various purposes. They don't refine matter to any degree of purity. Ignoring crystals, the purest substances seen since the Big Bang have been made in human smelters.

Ultimate Reshaping?

We've gotten cleverer in manipulating matter since the Bronze Age. Lots of new tools, products, and processes to Reshape(Matter) have emerged. The "final" step might be the Diamond Age of Neil Stephenson, "smelting" carbon into diamond with nanotechnology. The placement of every atom of matter exactly where you want it might qualify as a new *alt.age*, with respect to man's relationship with inert matter. This is the ultimate exactness in the Reshape(Inert.Matter) method. Reshape(Living.Matter) covers genetic manipulation. There's plenty of potential for a new *alt.age* in that method, too.

Information

INFORMATION is the fifth element of the Universe. Life can't live without it. The impact of information over our lives has increased over the ages. Stone Age individuals stored and transmitted information within family and band (mainly). Information from outside rarely affected them. They adopted memes from neighboring bands in a network of shared behaviors that characterized that *People*. They rarely adopted memes from other peoples. Kings and emperors made interactions between peoples more common. Money made trading promises between peoples easier. Writing meant the information that affected you could come from farther away in SPACE or TIME. We didn't get bounty posters until the Age of Plenty, though. Now a digital presence that surrounds us could empower a more modern form of bounty hunting, among other things. INFORMATION has powered new Tribes of the Age of Plenty. The impact of INFORMATION, in breadth and scope, will almost certainly become *more* important in our lives.

Analytic temporal reduction

The aspects of INFORMATION in focus here are *Memory*, *Models*, and *Promises*. Memories are of the past. The present is a model of the universe in the head of every brainy critter. Each critter's behavior depends on their model and their memories, including genetically remembered instinctive behaviors. Agreements are promises to behave in the future.

Memories

Dawkin's Replicator

Information didn't have much impact on the universe until life emerged, except at the quantum level, whatever that means. There were no mechanisms for storing or using information until DNA or its simpler grandfather emerged. The universe was as dumb as rocks, an informational Stone Age, literally. Sage Dawkins called the breakout critter the Replicator. A stack of chemicals that can replicate itself carries that informational pattern into the future. It could fill up the ocean. Who was to stop it? Eventually, one of its grandkids made a replication mistake that survived, and a second species emerged. Its grandkids evolved and ate Grandpa. That became the standard natural selection outcome. Unsuccessful information patterns do not survive. The grandkids developed RNA eventually. RNA still works but is in the slow lane of evolution (cloning). Both RNA and DNA remember only success. The system only remembers information patterns from critters that survive long enough to Spawn(). Patterns of atoms that fail have no impact on the system.

RNA defines the Clone Era

If we squash Earth history to a day, micro-life started around 6 a.m. when organic chemicals ordered themselves (self-assembled) into configurations that could replicate, hence the name Richard Dawkins gave to this first instance of life. RNA is the modern form of whatever string of chemicals the Replicator used to transmit information down the time stream. RNA is the information carrier in the Clone Era. The information needed to build a critter is duplicated. There will be mishaps in the duplication process, mostly fatal. Waiting for successful RNA cloning mishaps is a slow way to evolve. Still, the anaerobic algae that caused the Oxygen Catastrophe had an impact. Unfortunately, they enabled the next major change in life on Earth that saw them diminished to near insignificance. The new conditions forced anaerobic bacteria to retreat underground and into tin cans. A similar reduction in influence happened to the kings of Westphalia. It might happen to humans if we invent silicon life. Complex evolving systems are so unruly!

Sex increases the pace of evolution

At about 6 p.m., a new process emerged: *sex*. A new system of living things emerged, where patterns of information from *two* successful critters merged to create a non-identical offspring. DNA was the new information transmission device. The DNA

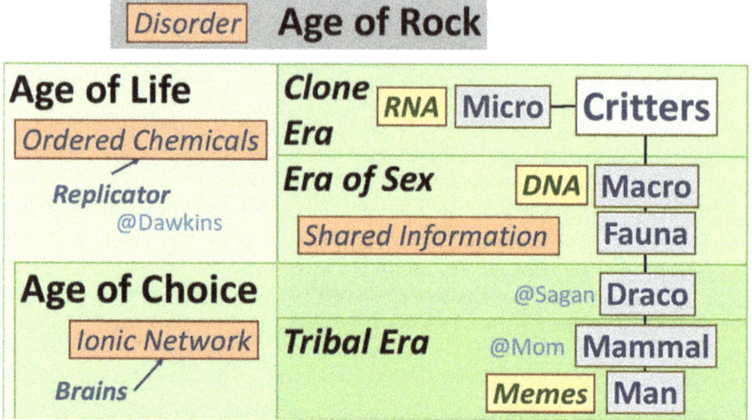

Great Moments in Information Storage

helix unzips and merges with another. The number of permutations exploded. The pace of evolution went through the roof. Multi-cellular critters evolved and packed their information into seed, spore, and egg. Of the three domains of Macro life (Flora, Fauna, and Funga), only Fauna has taken the *next* step in information storage. Only animals evolved *brains*.

A second information storage system emerges

Brains emerged to interpret photons but doubled as a memory storage device and tripled as a risk evaluation engine. Brains (and DNA) are composed of atoms, but the *Mind* is a network of electrical nodes linked by ions at the tips of the brain's neurons. DNA/RNA is real, physical matter. A Mind is a dynamic *phenomenon* like life itself. It stops working when Death cuts the energy off. The information is lost when the brain dies, no matter what the quantum physicists say. The Mind represents the *second* emergence of an information storage system on Earth, after RNA's grandpa, the Replicator. The Mind allows a critter to make choices based on what it has experienced in the past. That knowledge is lost when the critter dies–unless it's tribal. That's the whole point of culture! Elders use memes to transmit the knowledge they've acquired to the young in their tribes. A good meme will help the tribe survive and prosper. A bad meme can make it extinct. Try to avoid those.

Models of the Environment

The Age of Choice

The mind contains a model of the environment surrounding the critter. A micro-critter gets some sense of the environment by touch (which includes taste. Generally, the first thing a micro-critter does to anything that it touches is attempt to eat it.) A modern Micro is aware enough to use the Fight and Flight parameters of the Critter.React() method when touched.[58] Some Macro critters (the animals) have developed long range sensors and a mind (only the brainy animals) to interpret the incoming sensor data. That brain also developed a *memory* that remembers that critter's life experiences. Memory allows brainy critters to make choices beyond basic instincts. In *alt.age.information,* the Age of Life transitions to the Age of Choice. This age began with the *Brainiac* class of *Fauna*. Species of brainless fauna include the immobile filter-feeding animals, which we might class as vegetables here, though they lack the Eat(Photons) capability. It also excludes the slightly more mobile browsers like starfish or any spineless critter. To Critter.React(), we add the Brainiac.Choose() capability, which allows that the

---

[58] The Replicator would not have been so aware. Fungi aren't much better.

critter might act in ways *not* dictated by instinct alone. The Age of Choice might have started with the fish brain, because from that brain emerged the most primitive Mob on Earth, the *School*. Reptiles don't do much mobbing, though they'll swarm. Fish and reptiles can remember and learn as long as they live.

Mom teaches stuff

The young learn from mom in *Warm* species (birds and mammals). Mom is the first *Elder* of the first tribe on Earth. In a tribe other than *Family,* the pups can learn from any elder (when they listen! Memes are just suggestions. The learner must voluntarily weave the thought into their model of how the world works. When they become teens, they know it all and don't have to listen anymore.)

Symbolic information emerges

Human-specific methods of tribal information storage began with the first memes, propagated by oral history. In the universal sense, this was the first transmission of multi-generational INFORMATION by *verbal* symbols.[59] Verbal lore was good enough for 90% of human existence. All sorts of societies

---

[59] Mom (generic) doesn't symbolize. Her method of teaching is Demonstrate().

emerged, each with their own lore and behaviors. Beyond oral history, the written word and printing press generate *visible* symbols. Bits are electronic symbols. Each might be sub-eras within the Era of Memes.

The first meme

The first meme of record is the Legend of Og. An elder said to a youth, “Hey kid, Og died doing that!” Here, the elder is passing along critical information, a behavioral suggestion that will help the kid Survive() and Prosper(). We have no record of what “that” was that Og died doing, but we still honor his name. It also demonstrates that Og had a symbolic noise that recognized his uniqueness and referred to his individual self. Verbal *names* surely began before verbal memes.

Animal names?

Not many animals communicate beyond “Eek” = Danger! Are any on a path to *symbolic* verbal communication? Penguin moms can detect and home in on their chick’s voice, but that’s a noise the chick makes, not a name she gave it. Nonetheless, avians might be more advanced than mammals in verbal and listening skills. We assume all chimpanzees are named Ooh, but they may be more subtle than we know. A dolphin or whale might be the best candidate for a critter that creates names for its friends.

The first human name

There was an attempt in the 50's to teach chimps to talk with their mouths. Using their hands came later and worked far better. They tried to teach the word "cup" to a critter incapable of bilabial plosives. It had to hold its finger on its upper lip to hold its lips together against the air pressure to pop the "p" sound. Humans have evolved to hold our labia together to pop our p's and b's. We can make other distinctive noises, but bilabial plosives are particularly human. We share other consonants with the animal world. Even a dog can whine an "n". We share a throat vibrator with all animals to vocalize our vowels. We use the rest of our face to make different vowels. The default (resting face) vibration is the schwa. This isn't even on the list from A to Z. It may be more basic. Pre-humans might have used the schwa before they evolved to contort their faces and make the rest of the vowels. They became human when they added the bilabial plosives. The conclusion we draw from this is that the first truly human name might have been Bubba!

Alternate measures of humanity

Human names represent a huge jump in self-awareness and may be the first manifestation of language. There are several answers to the question, "When did humans separate from the other great apes?" Some say bipedalism. Some say tool-making. In the context of this section – the evolution of INFORMATION in the universe – the answer is language. Names may have been the first noises that meant something other than "Danger!".[60] Chirps and barks can convey the news that dangerous conditions now exist in the close vicinity of the mob. This is communication, not language, and practiced by many mobs. Names were likely the first nouns that emerged on Earth. That's why Nouns are capitalized in German and Java. The second noun on Earth was "Simba!", a *class* object that applies to all lions, whereas "Og" is a specific *instance* of a human object (deceased). These are two different examples of *emergence* within symbolic language, one categorical common noun and one specific instance of a proper noun. Verbs are a separate emergence. Add some adjectives and now you're talking.

---

60 Or "Mom!" or "Where is everybody?" or "Hey! Let's Spawn()"

Of sentience, self-awareness, and sapience

On the spectrum of consciousness, a minimal amount of animal *sentience* derives from an awareness of the environment beyond the animal. We define Animals possessing mental models and the ability to choose as *sentient* here. Lower animals simply react to touch. They are not very aware of their environment. Self-awareness comes later, roughly with warm blood and the phrase, "higher animals." One test involves a mirror placed in a jungle. That is useful for estimating the self-awareness of wild animals. For pets, just call their name. Not pet fish.

Models with a future

The next step up in the quality of consciousness is *sapience*. Normally, this is associated with Homo Sapiens, the thinking critter, but lots of critters think. That's how squirrels solve the various problems videographers set up for them. What makes human thinking special is thinking about the future. Predators might "lead the target," but that comes from experience, not any concept of future time. The future didn't matter until sapience emerged. No other animal was thinking that way and even fewer warm rocks.[61]

Promises, promises

Agreement is not assumed.

The future is the third temporal dimension of the INFORMATION element. Humans do several unique things with the future. We Predict() and Plan() and Promise(). Every agreement is a promise to act properly in the future. The standard Social Contract covers individual/tribe interactions, but individuals and tribes can also make promises to each other. When individuals or tribes don't keep their promises, there will be trouble.

The Money Meme

The beauty of *Money* is that it is a *portable* promise. Money has become more abstract over the ages. It was based on solid metal at first, then paper, now electronic bits. It's still a promise and promises make the world go around. Money provides a balancing mechanism between needs and desires. The government gets the first cut, to defend

61 or silicon chips (yet).

the border. The government had their hand in the till before there was a till. You paid in wheat back when. Emperors spread the Coin meme top-down. A bottom-up approach was attempted in the European Renaissance, with some 300 mints in France alone. Minting money is now a standard function of the *Country*. Paper money, where the state promises the value of the paper, is a more recent version of the Money meme. It requires more trust in the tribe than using coinage based on MATTER. If the state is honest, this can work. The hazard is that the country starts printing money it does not have. That sort of thing should lead to a loss of trust, but it is sneaky.

Predictions

A human can imagine the future and will sometimes talk about it. This communicates to their tribes their model of the most likely future. The tribe often finds this information useful. Predictions sold by soothsayers are less useful. The desire to know the future is built into the human genome. The opportunities for fraud are rife in the computer age with the development of fancy simulations. Computer output can convince the audience that the soothsayer has a handle on it. In fact, the sims usually have too many moving parts, a slew of assumptions, and it all depends on the input data, anyway. Currently, the most important of these efforts are climate models. They attempt to justify drastic changes that might just end the Age of Plenty. Decision-makers need to challenge the validity of their predictions. The methodology is fundamentally flawed. Complexity science implies that this approach will always suck.

Plans

Humans make plans to improve things or prevent them from getting worse. It starts with a *vision* of some favorable result. It becomes a *goal* when we consider the cost. A goal has two parts, maximize one good thing at minimum cost. Achieving the good thing requires an expenditure of resources. That's always TIME and usually money. The second step in planning is conjuring different courses of action that might achieve the goal. Choose one course and execute that. You should monitor progress during and after execution. That's the part that governments don't do very well. An individual does this many times a day on the little tasks and can have projects that take years. Some people have no long-term plans. There could be a Five-Bin chart for this attitude from the Carefree to Obsessive planners. At the tribal scale, attitude toward planning correlates closely with the Control Stack. The Soviets were great fans of five-year plans and top-down management.

Big plans

Tribes have bigger plans than individuals, such as ending poverty. It's easier to judge the success of little tasks. More complex tasks require care to ensure that the project actually supports the original goal. For posterity, we need to compare the results against the original goal. This doesn't happen often enough with government projects. Individuals doing their little projects are better at quality control than tribes in general. Size matters. The lack of an effective review process for public projects is a serious breach of good governance. We need better memes at that tribal level.

Communications issues

Backup vocals

We can divide the human Tribal Era into segments based on the improvements in information transfer that have emerged since we began to talk. *Vocals* are good enough for lore and memes and song. The tribe uses a succession of human minds to store INFORMATION and uses their voices to transmit it.[62] The first human art added *sight-based* information

[62] with Elder.Demonstrate() transmission for wordless techno-memes.

storage. The artist creates a model, a direct visual representation of an object (noun) important to him. (Verbs are tougher to convey but a *real* artist...) The Pictograph meme involved a direct mapping (to 2-D) of an object to its symbol. Phonetic symbols map not the object, but the sounds we string together to model the object. It's a model of a model, a major emergence. Phonetic writing supplanted the picto-commo meme everywhere it traveled. It was a better, more compact meme, if measured by the size of typewriter keyboard required.[63] The limited character set is also easier to learn, which makes literacy less the province of an intellectual elite.[64] However, phonetic writing has less potential to be artistic.

The writing epoch

Ink is more permanent than sound waves (by a lot), but words last in memory. Written INFORMATION is stored as ordered MATTER rather than as ionic patterns remembered by a succession of elders. This is not always an advantage. Lore is more reliable than the parlor game Telephone, where a story is whispered in a circle and mangled to the great amusement of all. Lore passers get to tell their tales more

---

[63] in Japan

[64] in China

than once. They can also tailor their missive to their audience. The Word is sometimes written in stone, therefore not as flexible as oral history. Which holds more truth? How does their truth compare to the Internet? The Computer Age uses bits to represent letters and .wav patterns to store sounds. This is more flexible than art or print or oral history, to the extent that software can rearrange the bits to produce the exact *opposite* of the original message. Our control over INFORMATION may have reached another emergent moment, the Age of Untrustworthy Information.

Life

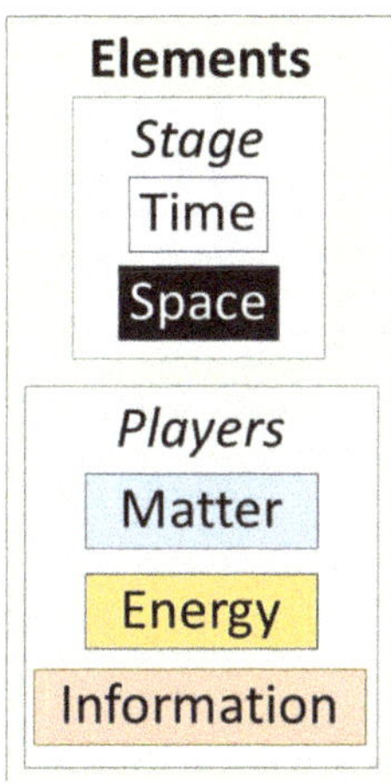

A Phenomenon of Complexity

Life is the most interesting *phenomenon* in the universe. It is the product of a universal tendency toward complexity, "If things can get more interesting, they will." [65] Living things can *react* to their environment. Before Life happened, the universe had only warm rocks, which seldom do anything as interesting. Lots of interesting things ensued when life emerged.

[65] Attributed to the Goddess Gaea, represented on Earth by Mother Nature

Life's components

My model reduces life to three ingredients, Matter, Energy, and Information and it operates in a universe composed of Space and Time. These five elements interact in interesting ways, especially after life emerges. The key to life becoming ever-more interesting is *evolution*, which happens to Species and Tribes. Individual critters don't evolve, though the smarter ones *adapt* and get better at surviving as they age (until they don't). The distinction is sharp here between evolution and adaptation. Evolution is the long-term reaction to changes in the environment by a *Group* of critters. Individual brainy critters *adapt* and learn better how to survive. This information is lost when the critter dies unless the critter is *tribal*. The emergence of tribal memory (lore) is just the third way to preserve information since life emerged, after DNA and brains. Tribal memory can immortalize the knowledge of individuals as long as the tribe shall live.

Groups: Can't describe Life on Earth without them

Groups (species, tribes, and uncultured mobs) are *immortal* in comparison to the individual critters that populate them. That gives groups some behaviors very different from critters. They are a different expression of life's evolution. But there are some characteristics and abilities that individual critters and groups of critters share. They both "want" to Survive() and Prosper(). Groups are very sticky survivors compared to critters.

A model of a simulation (of a model)

An object-oriented (Java-like) simulation of my model of life assigns *methods* to its *objects* to give them lifelike capabilities. The top-level object is Life itself, abbreviated LivingThing below. Java has *inheritance*, which means Mother Nature and all her children, real (physical) *Critters* or "phenomenal" *Groups*, want to Survive() and Prosper(). All critters Eat(), Spawn(), and Die().

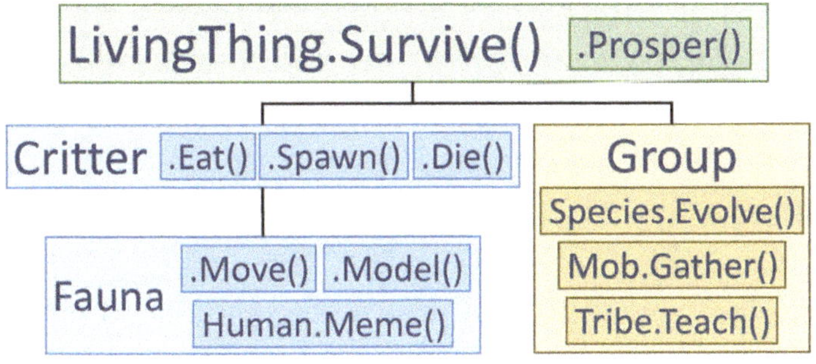

Object.Verb() syntax

Animals have additional capabilities unavailable to plants, fungus, or micro critters, though not all animals, as currently defined, can move and only the brainy ones have a model of their environment in their heads. Humans get their own methods of behavior, including transmitting memes (due to our invention of "words of wisdom"). Groups of critters have different capabilities. For instance, groups don't eat or die. Species evolve. So do tribes. Mortal critters *adapt* to changes in their environment during their lives but don't evolve. Mother Nature is a construct of INFORMATION, not ENERGY nor MATTER. She is a set of rules that allow her children, both species and tribes, to evolve and become more interesting.

Life Code

Pseudo-Java

Life is a phenomenon, not an object made of physical MATTER. Java is an *object*-oriented computer language, so we use *LivingThing* as the top-level object in LifeSim. Group and Critter and Human are also generic *class* objects, the children of classes higher on the Tree of Life. Classes are notional, idealized templates for real physical objects. The real thing is an *instance* of the class. Within the class Car, each physical instance has a

Vehicle Identification Number. The *class* Car doesn't need one, but it has one just to make it easier to fill in the form when a real car comes off the production line. The Class is a generic template, with slots for Make and Model and other characteristics that make each real instance of Car unique. You became a new instance of the *Human* class when you were born. You.Survive() until You.Die(). Those are two of the *methods* (verbs) that apply to all living critters. Inside the method's parentheses, that kind of life activity might have *parameters* (adverbs) for a special case such as Micro.Eat(H_2S) for thermal vent critters.

Class act

The pseudo-code below *declares* the top-level class in LifeSim, my model of life on Earth. *Critters* and *Groups* of critters are separate types of living things, but they share some aspects and capabilities of being alive. They React() to changes in their environment. Unliving matter (abbreviated rocks) don't do anything so interesting.[66] The class declaration below creates the most generic object in LifeSim. The only thing known about a living thing is whether it is still alive. Set Extant=0 when an instance of

[66] Phase changes are the most interesting things non-living matter can do.

species goes extinct, or a critter dies, or a mob or tribe disperses.

Top Level LifeSim Object: The Living Thing

The pseudo-code in italics below exemplifies the declaration of the top-level class in LifeSim. All living things, both Critters and Groups of critters, have this single characteristic (attribute) in common and these five capabilities (methods).

```
class LivingThing extends Object {
//Attribute    Data Type    Comment
  Extant       Boolean      // Still there?
//Methods
  React( ) {sim code}       // Adapt or Evolve
  Remember( ) {...}         // Use DNA or brains
  Survive( ) {...}          // You need this
  Compete( ) {...}          // You must
  Prosper( ) {...}  }       // You desire this
```

What living things do for a living

All instances of LivingThing want to Survive() and Prosper() and must Compete() to do so. They can do so because they Remember() the past. Species use DNA to remember *patterns* of information that have succeeded in the past. Critters with brains remember past *events*.

Critters

All living organisms on Earth, from micro-life to plants to the higher animals, fit under the category *Critter*. All critters are composed of MATTER from the low end of the periodic table. The atoms arrange themselves into rickety stacks that can store energy harvested from the environment. They can use this energy for maintenance, growth, and procreation. In fact, that's their job. The entire life cycle of some critters is Critter.Eat() > Critter.Mature()[67] > Critter.Spawn() > Critter.Die(). That's life. That's what all the people say.

What is the meaning of life?

For what purpose do we exist? The standard secular explanation involves the Critter.Spawn() method. Critters exist only to make more critters. But a more basic purpose resides within the Critter.Mature() method. The critter grows and puts on mass. This is in the form of *ordered* MATTER, organized from

---

[67] Maturity = doubling in size for micro-life or a much higher multiplier for seed, spore, or egg

the chaos of molecules it has ingested.[68] Most of this newly organized matter is doomed to be ingested, especially those critters that were "born to be eaten." They live only to enable "higher" critters to live. At the top of the chain is the human critter, which can imagine a higher purpose in life than simply breeding more humans or getting eaten. All critters bequeath their *genetic* information to the next generation. Tribal critters like humans bequeath their *learned* information. Tribes have their own specific purpose in life–to preserve wisdom.

Critter Basics

Energy storage

Rickety stacks of atoms from the low end of the table of elements, it turns out, can store Energy and retrieve it later. Not all combinations are stable (and some are explosive) but energy storage is a big deal. The surface of Earth and the cores of supernovae are the only places we know it happens. Most of Earth's stored energy (originally photons from the sun) is in the form of coal. Individual critters use stored energy to maintain the critter's structure as part of the Survive(Maintain) method. The critter

[68] This is all part of Gaea's tendency to bring order to the universe.

needs extra energy to grow big enough to reproduce, and more to grow the next generation egg/seed/spore. After producing successful replacements, critters can die. Their carefully arranged atoms can no longer oppose entropy after system shutdown. Things go downhill from there. There's still energy left in the arrangement of the atoms in their bodies. Fungi and Micros can scavenge some energy from the remains, but entropy wins in the end. Life can only defy the downhill tendency of entropy as an active, dynamic process. We are always running in place, maintaining our rickety stack of energetic atoms. Even when resting, we are, at the molecular level, quite busy.

Critters fight Entropy

Critter.Survive(Repair) is one key to what makes Life special. All the repair mechanisms in cells/micros and larger critters replace chaos with order. These activities oppose the universal trend toward chaos called entropy. Entropy tends to disperse energy and order. We can only *reverse* entropy if we are extremely lucky. We can *overcome* entropy, however, at least locally. Events that create order, rather than disperse it, can happen in a system with an excess of energy. This only happens in *open* systems. The Earth is not a closed system, as it gets ENERGY from the sun. With respect to this, the Egyptians got it right by venerating Ra.

Critter class declaration

The pseudo-code below (do not try to compile it!) describes the generic critter of Earth. Critters will *inherit* the Survive(), Compete(), and other methods from above.

```
class Critter extends LivingThing {
//Attribute      Data Type      Comment
   Mass          Float          // Groups have no mass
   Species       String         // Assigned at birth
//Methods
   Eat( ) {...}                 // Obtain energy
   Mature( ) {...}              // Grow up enough to spawn
   Spawn( ) {...}               // Prime Directive
   Die( ) {...}    }            //Make room for better kids
```

Critter, a LivingThing with Mass

The Critter (class) inherits (through the *extends* keyword) all the capabilities of all living things, its *parent* class. Every living critter wants to live long and prosper. It *needs* to survive and *desires* to prosper. Each critter desires to replace itself. Consider this an order from the Species, enforced by instinct. Every critter is composed of physical MATTER and has physical mass, called an *attribute* in Java or a *characteristic* in other object-oriented simulation languages. The critter's species (or any other group) doesn't have any mass. Attributes record the current status of the *instances* of each critter in the simulation. Every critter is born with mass and a very basic set of capabilities for dealing with the world. These *methods* are Eat(), Mature(), Spawn(), and Die(). These activities comprise the entire lifestyle of the earliest and simplest critters on Earth. It was a while before they could Play(). Critters exist to create more critters like themselves. Micro-critters create critters *exactly* like themselves by cloning. Sexy critters take a chance that their offspring might be an improvement. Sex allows wider variation, so half of the kids *will* be better. It's one of Gaea's best tricks.

Critters of the Micro world unite!

```
class Micro extends Critter {
  Spawn(RNA) {...} }           // Clones
```

Big critters like sex

Besides size, the big difference between Micro and Macro critters is how they Spawn(). Micros Spawn() by cloning. Macros spawn with a parameter that indicates two critters are involved. Macros have sex! More specifically, they have sex organs, which have (lots) more than one cell. Multi-cellular life was a huge emergent event in the history of life on Earth. Microbial mats or biologicals film don't count. All the critters in such *Swarms* are exactly (more or less) the same. The key factor in "multi-cellular life" is not the number of cells but that the cells are different, like skin and bone. Within Macro-life cells specialized and critters evolved separate organs, an emergent event like the later Division of Labor meme. Each macro critter is an integrated system of cells and organs. Micros are integrated systems of organelles.

Macro critters, another win for complexity

The Macro class has subclasses Flora, Fauna, and Funga. Flora and some micro-critters are distinguished by the Eat(Photons) parameter. Powering life with solar energy was another huge emergence in the history of Earth. The first critters ate energetic chemicals like hydrogen sulfide. Access to a completely different source of Energy will always be a big deal. Early Micros produced enough oxygen to cause the Oxygen Catastrophe. That event supercharged life on Earth, increasing the *rate* of emergences and the number of possible paths to interesting futures. One of those paths led to class Flora, which along with Funga don't do much interesting with respect to group activity. Only animals form social groups, which is an emergence of great interest in this model.

Four major Domains of Critter

All living organisms on Earth are of the class Critter. The oldest subcategory of critter is the Micro-critters. For about two-thirds of the history of life on Earth, they were the *only* critters. Then they got together, and Macro (multi-celled) critters emerged. These became the Flora, Fauna, and Funga domains of today. Carolus Linnaeus, the Swedish taxonomer and sage, categorized the Animal and Vegetable kingdoms. The Fungal kingdom is from Piers Anthony, author of the science fiction Omnivore series and a Minor Prophet here. His planet Nacre had no fauna but mobile (and brainy) fungi to take their place, "proving" that animals aren't required for a functional eco-system. Plant life (microbial and airborne on Nacre) stores energy. Various forms of mobile fungus feed on the manna from above and recycle. Fungi still have the Recycle() function here on Earth.[69] Earth animals, though, are superfluous freeloaders! We simply steal the energy that plants store. We use a portion of that energy to move

[69] and some are quite tasty, he said, unapologetically.

around. You will not find the Move() method in the declarations for classes *Flora* or *Funga*. Only mobile animals form Mobs. (Micro critters can move but don't form mobs, so aren't very interesting.)

Domain methods (pass down attributes: extant, mass)

The four subsets of living critters are Micro, Flora, Fauna, and Funga. Each has a unique set of methods or parameters for handling the adventure of life but have no new attributes. Extant and Mass (inherited from parent classes) are common to all domains. We only define Animals in higher detail. Here the Animal class gets the ability to move, which its future instances will need to follow the Mob.

Macro branch (domain/kingdom)

```
class Macro extends Critter   {// Multi-cellular
  Spawn(ShareDNA) {...}       }// Come together
```

Flora, daughter of Macro

```
class Plant extends Macro   { // Can't move
  Spawn(Seed) {...}
  Eat(Photon) {...}           // Critical eating habit
  React(Track) {...}          }// Track the sun
```

Funga, the recycler

```
class Fungus extends Macro        {
 Spawn(Spore) {...}
 Eat(Booze) {...}               } // Fermentation
```

Fauna, the Animal kingdom

```
class Animal extends Macro    {
 Spawn(Egg) {...}            // Sexiest parameter[70]
 Move( ) {...}               } // All Mobs move
class Carnivore extends Animal {
 Hunt( ) {...} } // alone
class Herbivore extends Animal {
 Gather( ) {...} } // includes Veggiesaurus
```

Only brainy critters join Mobs

A second requirement for forming an instance of class *Mob*, after mobility, is being able to recognize your mates. (Myopic critters can still blunder into a *Swarm*.)[71] At a minimum, the recognition of a fellow group member requires an eye, an optic nerve, and a brain with a *Mind*.

---

[70] Author's personal preference

[71] Swarm: A temporary Mob, including two (or more) critters that gather only to mate.

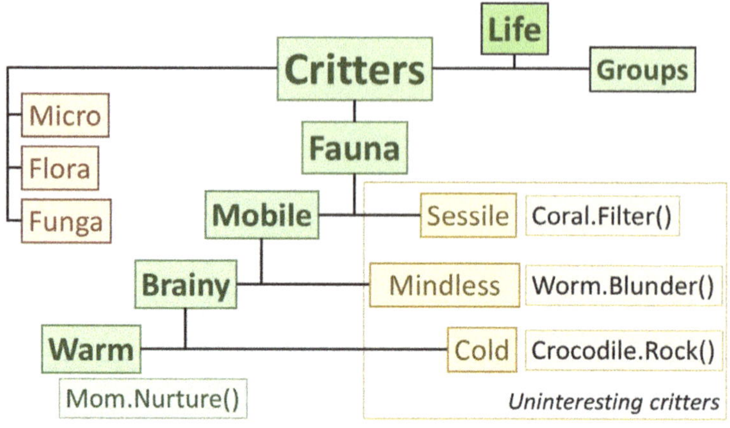

Critters of Interest: Warm Fauna

The mind processes incoming photons into a coherent model of the critter's environment. Remote sensing is a huge step up for a critter's situational awareness. Before that, critters had only touch to trigger Critter.React(). In the succession of interesting things that have happened since the Big Bang, the mental model, the *Mind*, ranks high. Touch is only skin deep. Critters need remote sensors to get beyond that. Structurally, any Critter with a spinal cord and a clever knot of nerves at one end is "mindful". That knot can interpret incoming signals well enough to recognize members of its own species and form a Mob. The Mob.Gather() capability is valid for fish and higher. Insects and lower can still mindlessly Swarm().

Bonus capability

Another capability, besides recognizing your mob mates, emerged from the knot of nerves called the Dragon brain by Sage Sagan.[72] At first, the animal brain was a signal interpreter to model the world around it. It then developed into a memory storage device. The past began to make a difference, for the second time in the history of the universe.[73] Critters now can Remember() previous experiences, which influences what behavior they choose when reacting. Memory feeds a risk analysis engine that allows the critter to do more than the default response, Critter.React(Flinch). The next significant step in the ability of a critter to use INFORMATION, after learning from its own past, is learning from *another* critter's past. That's what tribes are for.

Brainy critters: Capable of forming Mobs (but loners allowed)

The code below describes the capabilities that come with brain power, mainly the ability to choose. The evolution of complex brains triggered the Age of Choice. Insects may have tiny brains, but not a

---

[72] We prefer Shark brain.

[73] The first was the Replicator from Sage Dawkins. It remembered itself.

Mind. They don't remember or make choices. They only have instinct.

```
class Brainiac extends Animal     {
//Attribute    Data Type    Comment
  Social       Boolean      // Might join a Mob
//Methods
  Model( ) {...}               // To spot Mob mates
  Remember(Event) {...}        // To gain wisdom
  React(Choose) {...}}         // After a risk analysis
```

Life choices

A critter with a brain can makes choices, like joining a *Herd* (subclass of *Mob*). All social, brainy critters have an instinctive mobbing behavior. Critters join a school/flock/herd for help in the ever-present tasks of obtaining energy and avoiding becoming energy for predators. Solo species like tigers took a different path. DNA writes the choice to gather into the social critter's instincts. All critters, brainy or not, have instincts written into their genes that "dictate" how they behave. The critter's personal memories are the other major input to its behaviors. If you're tribal, those "lived experiences" include what you've learned from Mom or any other elders.

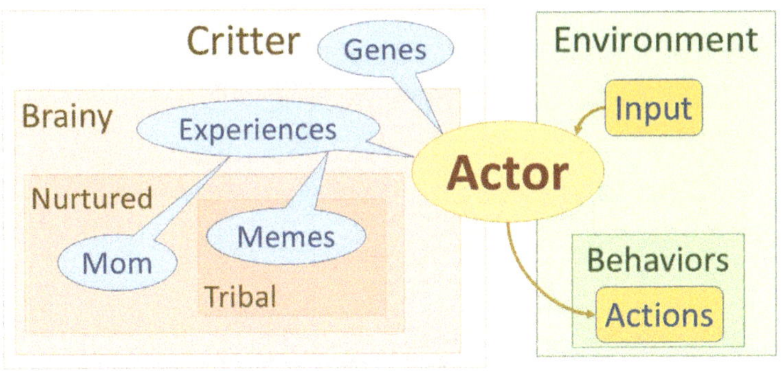

Why Critters do what they Do

Smarter critters get more choices.

The simplest brainy critters (~fish) use *instinct* 99.99% of the time they Choose().[74] Seldom do they use previous personal *experience*. Snakes and frogs aren't known for learning new tricks, either. That ratio of instinct to wits changes with smarter critters, reaching 50/50 with humans.[75] Wisdom accrues as a brainy critter ages. Its mental model of How the World Works improves over time. "Higher" animals can, additionally, learn from the experiences of Mom or the elders of the tribe. Experiences are

74 Source: completely made up

75 This is known because nobody has won the Nature/Nurture debate.

what you've done yourself, but technically include what you've *seen* Mom do or *heard* from the elders. Non-human tribes don't talk, so the young see the elders *demonstrate* their wisdom.

The Model of the world in your head

A brain gives a critter a view of the environment. In two parts, the environment consists of the background and surprises. The background doesn't change, though should a critter Move(), a slice of the background moves offscreen and a new slice appears. If the background indeed changes, it's a surprise because every *event* is a surprise. The status quo assumes that things won't change. That's as far ahead as most critters "think." Events can be beneficial or harmful to the survival of the critter. The response to the event might or might not help the situation. The trick is to remember what worked and what didn't, which is what brains are for. A critter with a clever brain might *anticipate* an event. The cat anticipates dinner because he has seen similar events happen before and incorporated them in its model of how the world works. Dinner is not a surprise. Anticipation is a weak form of prediction, which apparently requires a human-sized brain. We assume the mental model of any non-human critter is rooted entirely in the past. Humans have a lock on the futures market.

Warm-blooded critters are the best moms

The pseudo-code below describes the unique capabilities of the "higher" animals, birds and mammals. Both classes of critters share the life activities below, actions never taken by frogs and snakes, much less worms or lilies.

```
class Warm extends Brainiac {// Higher animal
//Methods
  React(Emote) {...}          // Love it or hate it
  Nurture( ) {...}            // To start a Family
  Play( ) {...}               // Physical training[76]
  Vocalize( ) {...}      }    // Mob warning calls[77]
```

Dragons plus a limbic brain layer

Fish and reptiles barely qualify as Brainiacs with their Dragon/Shark brains. Surrounding that, in the Sagan model, is the mammalian brain. We also grant this level of brain power is to avians. This assumes warm-bloodedness has something to do

---

[76] and social bonding

[77] plus bonding howls and coos

with it. The gap between brain sizes is noticeable at the reptile/bird interface. The extra brain mass layered over the shark brain allows several new functions like curiosity, emotions, and creativity. Turtles and snakes aren't known for those traits. Higher animals are those that Nurture() their young. This behavior emerged in mammals and birds long ago and set the conditions for the nature/nurture debate of today. Crocodile moms and cichlids (fish) get partial credit for hiding the pups in their mouths. Birds and mammals Play(), which sharpens the kitten's claw delivery system. Among social animals, play helps the kids make friends among the local mob.

Nurture = Protect() + Feed() + Teach()

Nurture started with a mom who protected and fed her chicks. Moreover, Mom *taught* them, the first instance of life experiences being transferred to the next generation. It's a long way from memes, but it's a start. Family, the oldest kind of tribe, starts with Mom. Dad is optional. Birds are better dads than mammals. Scholars estimate 90% of avians Marry() vs 5% of mammals.[78]

[78] Source: two hits

Mob voices

Individual critters make a variety of noises for various purposes. Some of them involve mob behavior. Mom calls to the cubs. Birds chirp to keep the flock together in funky terrain. (Fish don't do that.) Howling at the moon is a classic *bonding* behavior in the audible range. The most common vocal mob activity across all warm species is shouting, "Danger!" Snakes don't shout. Reptiles and amphibians aren't very social, and some vocalize only to mate. (The frog army and garden snake orgy are *Swarms*, not permanent *Mobs*.) Many reptiles (but not many fish) make noise, but few vocalize for the social reasons listed in the //comment. Vocalization allows one member of the Mob to warn the others, perhaps the best reason for joining the mob.

Mob communications

The warm critter that is shouting conveys to the Mob that a surprise has just entered its worldview. This is important new input from the environment, communicated from a single set of eyes to other critters in the local mob. This is one basic reason that mobs work, communicating INFORMATION from one to many. Humans expanded the information pipeline when we started saying more than "Eek." We can comment on a much wider variety of topics now. It's still a transfer of the contents of one's personal mental model to other members of the mob.

Man of memes

The critter in focus here, of course, is the human animal, the talking ape, the meme and tool maker. We have an instinct to socialize and a mom and a dad. We inherit all the other powers and characteristics of our parent classes. We're like every other critter in that we want to survive and prosper. We have remote sensors and a photon interpretation center inside our heads, like any brainiac. We're warm.

```
class Human extends Warm{// Maker of memes
//Attribute      Data Type       Comment
  Possessions    List[Thing]     // Own it
//Methods
  Model(Future) {...}            //Plan, promise, predict
  Nurture(Dad) {...}             //Add Dad to the Family
  Reshape(Matter) {...}          // Maker of Tools
  Vocalize(Symbols) {...}        } // Maker of Words
```

The model of the world in human heads includes a concept of the future. Time is one of the five basic elements of the Universe. A relationship with a new "region" of one of the Big Five is a major emergence.[79] Man is the only critter that makes plans for a *better* future. Animals will seek a good time, food first and comfort next. Humans make plans for future good times, which includes promises to each other to work in concert to achieve a good time. Our capability to imagine the future is inherently human but variously enabled. Its influence on each of us–how much we actually plan ahead or even think ahead–ranges from Carefree to Disciplined. Homer Simpson represents an individual "living in the moment." He is among the 2.5% crazies, which he Survive()s only through the magic of animation. Carefree tribes have low survivability rates. "Live for the Moment" is a bad meme if the whole tribe catches it. Note that a Disciplined tribe doesn't have to be Authoritarian. The Discipline axis and Control Stack might be totally *uncorrelated* (90 degrees from each other, if you're graphic about it).

The Dad parameter

Humans have the Dad parameter, which adds an Elder to pass down family traditions. For 90% of human existence, Dad was also an elder of two other tribes, the local Band and the People. As a band

[79] The Science Channel guy listed intelligence as the third great emergence. Forward thinking!

member, Dad can also instruct the other kids in the group. These are hands-on lessons, mostly involving hunting tricks. He transmits the people's memes less consciously through its Lore. This includes religion and Sagas, a subclass of Story owned by the People. Dad also demonstrates gestures (non-verbal behaviors) that distinguish his people from others. We would need to declare the Dad parameter for most bird species. They're better at it than mammals.

Noisy critters

Humans vocalize a wide range of symbolic noises.[80] We receive strings of such noises and process them in a sound interpretation center equivalent to our optical sensor package. We can transmit our version of an Event to other humans vocally. We can also transmit a false version of the story for selfish reasons. Successful societies find memes to discourage that. We employ a more benign derivative when we vocalize a joke. Jokes are little lies intended to put a dent in someone's mental model for a moment.

80 *Humanoids* would not have the Vocalize(Symbols) capability.

Possessions

We keep more stuff than any other animal. We are born with nothing but eventually need a list to name all our possessions. We pass them on to our kids in the Family.Bequeath() method. We will assume this behavior to be instinctive until we find some Stone Age society that doesn't have this habit. Every society that had a king had a special version for the throne. The king and other noble families also had a Bequeath(Rights) parameter. They inherited privileged behaviors not available to the common folk.

What critters do

Eat(), Mature(), Spawn(), and Die()

The prime directive encoded into any critter is to multiply. You must Survive() long enough and Prosper() enough to Mature() enough[81] to Spawn() the next generation. Then you can Die(), which is necessary because immortality is an evolutionary dead end. These tasks, except the last, require energy. All critters must Eat() to obtain that energy. Flora.Eat(Photons) and store that Energy as carbs,

[81] Mature() order of magnitude: Micro double, Fauna/Funga/Flora 100-1000x seed/spore/egg mass

shorthand for energetic, organic, edible MATTER. Carbs are the default (no parameter) food for anything but plants. Micros that Eat(H_2S) eat inorganic MATTER. As a link between the Replicator and the first photosynthesizing critters, they did their part.

Higher activities

Once sated with ENERGY, critters mostly rest, but the smarter critters find other things to do. Warm blooded critters Nurture() and Play(). These activities and Eat() take up most of their waking day. Nurture and play are group activities that help the family and/or mob survive. Eating and sleeping are Me Time. Nurturing is Family Time. Any activity that contributes to group bonding is Social Time. That would include any time the Yak.Circle() or the whale pod blows a bubble net. Tribal Time is any time you devote to fulfilling your tribal duties. People in healthy tribes with a lot of Tribal Time on their ledger get bigger funerals.

Critter budgets

Life is a gift. What do critters do with it? We can reduce the analysis to how they spend their time and their energy. Much of the energy is spent in the background in maintenance and repair. Mobile critters spend energy in the pursuit of the next dose of energy, i.e., lunch. The time spent in pursuit of food doesn't count as free time. Free time is for the pursuit of anything else, broadly justified under Prosper(). Physical prosperity results in the critter growing large enough to spawn. Mental prosperity covers intellectual and emotional pursuits, including the satisfying activity of doing absolutely nothing because you have met all your (survival) *needs* and (prosperity) *desires*.

Birds but not Bees

Our focus on mobile, brainy, social critters leaves out a few interesting critters. Octopi have a fine brain but aren't very social. If octopi formed permanent mobs, they'd (probably) soon be declared tribes, when the elders start teaching tricks to their young to help them Survive() and Prosper(). At the other end are ants and bees, very social but not too bright. Here, insects are considered mindless, totally instinctive, and unable to Choose(). Insects still form interesting groups, however. Hives and colonies were among the first systems studied in complexity science (along with species and cities). Hives are, compared to human societies, quite boring. Hive behaviors haven't changed much since spit got sticky. Hives aren't evolving very fast these days. Still, this "primitive" social behavior marks a minor *emergence* in the history and variety of Life on Earth. The dance of the bees hints at how far complexity can develop along a very different branch of life. Bees may not have brains, but they have something they use for one. A fly's eyes aren't connected to anything we'd call a brain, but they do connect to its React() button and rather well. It takes time to send the signal to the brain, process it, and get instructions from central control. The eyespot of some micros might be even faster. Evolution has a lot of pathways and tradeoffs. Some paths are more productive in the interesting things they lead to. Brains are slow but have great potential. Per Gaea's instructions, life tries to keep it interesting.

Your Personal Schedule

How did you spend your day?

Time is your most precious and flexible resource. Most of us spend some time working to feed ourselves. For many humans that takes forty hours per week, but we also get enough money to seek comfort and Play(). Forty hours should take care of food, clothing, shelter and the entertainment budgets. The money comes from your social contract with your employer, so counts as tribal time. Part of this time (exactly equal to taxes/gross pay), you are actually working for your several government tribes. The rest of the day is Me Time by default. You reduce this and add to your Tribal Time by supporting your specific tribes. Family Time is a big-ticket item. Church costs an hour per week or so. Hobby clubs and bowling leagues gather to Play(). These *communities*[82] don't ask much, just your time, sometimes a fee. You are just supposed to show up on time, behave yourself, and Bond().

How do you prosper() from your Tribes?

People gather for more serious purposes than Play(). These fall under the Advocate() method, an umbrella concept that includes charities, political parties, and professional societies. The last of these is most directly related to personal prosperity, but you prosper at least emotionally from the others. If you don't, you should quit that tribe. It's your time. Spend it on yourself or with others. If it's just you and your friends horsing around, that's Social Time. Your personal mob doesn't qualify as a tribe. It lacks immortality. But they can still exclude you from their circle for bad behavior.

---

[82] Communities are the weakest form of Tribe.

The Social Contract

Members obtain benefits from their tribes. In return, members dedicate their TIME, ENERGY, and INFORMATION to support tribal goals. This is the boilerplate *Social Contract,* which is, these days, quite formal for any human tribe larger than family. Even your bowling league has bylaws, to which you will submit or you're out. This is basic tribal behavior, but some mobs discourage bad behavior, too, often administered by an Alpha critter. One basic power of the Mob, including all tribes, is to Exclude() existing or potential new members.

The information commitment meme

Your contribution to the tribe usually consists of three of the five basic elements of the universe, your TIME, your ENERGY, and your INFORMATION. The tribe seldom requires you to offer your physical MATTER.[83] You must commit some TIME to your tribe, or you are useless. You can use part of your paycheck instead of your physical presence. The money came from the Company Time you spent previously. The tribe might expect you to commit more ENERGY than just sitting around bonding, but it is hard *not* to expend

[83] Head shaving clerics and penitent Yakuza excepted.

energy. The interesting part, as usual, is the INFORMATION component. Your experience counts. The tribe expects you to use your experience, talent, and creativity in support of the tribal goal. Successful tribes have a meme that encourages you to give all you got. In contrast is the Skate meme, where you do as little as you can get away with. Tracking this attitude could be an effective measure of the health of a tribe. Slackers don't Prosper() and might not Survive().

Groups of Critters

The focus of this analysis is on the *Tribes of Man*, how they behave and your personal connection to the tribes you inhabit. Tribes are cultured mobs, which are any permanent group of mobile, brainy, social critters.

Groups, Mobs, and Tribes

The Species is an *involuntary* collection of critters, united by their interoperable DNA. There are also various Mobs of *social* critters, including herd, school, and gaggle. A mob is a *voluntary*

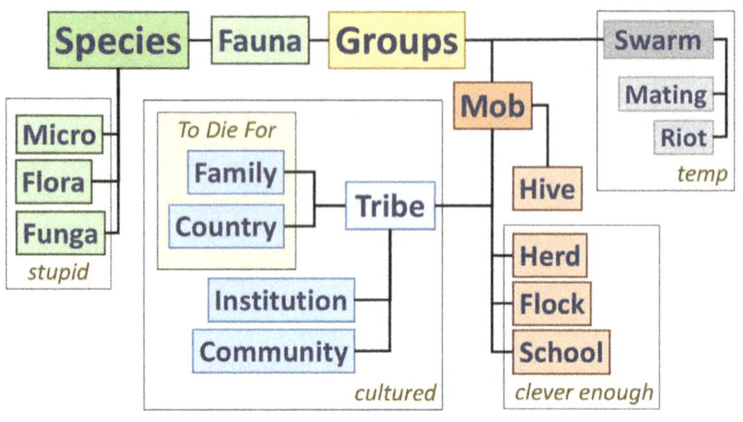

Only Animals form Groups

association of critters. Every herd has its mavericks. They get eaten first, which is why herds work, but it is still the individual critter's choice. Tribes have a culture, sometimes called an "institutional memory." Mobs and species got no culture.[84] Man has more *kinds* of tribes than any other critter. Family and Country are "To Die For". Your church, company, or baseball team do not require that level of loyalty.

[84] In a Brooklyn accent

Mating is a good excuse to Swarm.

A temporary group is a *Swarm*, even when it's just the two of us together forever. Mating is an excellent reason to get together from the perspective of the species. Every animal species uses instinct to make that happen. Most species swarm and disperse. Rarely, critters pair up and stick together for life. That's still not multi-generational, so a marriage is a "temporary" swarm, unlike a Family.

Characteristics of Groups

Species and mobs are the two basic *Groups* in this model of life. Tribes are just a clever sort of Mob. Species and mobs share some basic characteristics.

1. Groups want to grow. This is a positive feedback loop. If you don't have this drive, you go extinct. Species want to increase their range. Mobs want to increase their numbers. Corporations want to grow their market share.

2. Groups have a We/They relationship with *non-members* of the Group. Non-members are treated differently. Species won't mate with Them and might eat

Them. Territorial mobs recognize and fight Them or establish *borders* with Them.

3. Groups don't weigh anything. They have no physical matter beyond that of their members. They are composed entirely of INFORMATION. For species, the information is packed into a range of compatible DNA patterns. The mob mentality is an *agreement* to stick together. Sociability is written into the DNA along with other instincts that permit that species to survive and prosper.

4. Groups are immortal–at least they don't die of old age. The Mob.Survive(Replenish) method replaces the individual units within the group. The equivalent Critter. Survive(Repair) mechanism doesn't convey immortality.

5. Individuals behave differently in Groups. Individual fish in a school decide where to go based on their neighbors. Solo fish, in contrast, go wherever they want. Stampeding cattle bash though things they would normally avoid. Peaceful people do violent things in a riot (aka swarm).

Characteristics of Species

Species are not voluntary groups.

Membership in a species is not voluntary. If species had social contracts, they might read, "Mate with your own species or you're out of the gene pool!" But there is no interaction between any individual and its species, much less a contract. The species does nothing active to help any critter survive or prosper. It gives no service, so the individual owes it nothing. This is far different from other kinds of groups. Herds offer protection and deserve some level of loyalty in return. Tribes offer a wider range of services.

Origins in Complexity Science

Species are the original poster child for *complex adaptive systems*. Species are composed of independent agents that Die(), but the species lives on. Evolution *requires* that the individual members of the group die. They are replaced by the next generation, some of which will be a little smarter or faster or whatever than their parents. Evolution requires memory, which DNA provides. Species have a built-in positive feedback loop that encourages growth. Every species will expand to its natural range and may Evolve() beyond it.

Code for Groups

The pseudo-code below describes the Group class, which includes species and mobs. The one thing they have in common is that they can cease to exist even though they are "immortal". The Expire() method includes code for an instance of species or mob to die horribly in some currently unspecified manner. (Technically, due to the rules of data encapsulation, the volcano or other event "calls" the Group.Expire() method, and the group kills itself.)

```
class Group extends LivingThing          {
 Expire( ) {set Extant = 0}
 // "Death" for a generic group          }
```

Code for Species

The pseudo-code below describes the genetically inspired groups called Species. Species inherit the need to survive and desire to prosper from the top. They react to the challenges the environment throws at them by evolving. They can die, but in a manner far different from the death of a critter (except for the last member of a species).

```
class Species extends Group          {
//Attribute   Data Type    Comment
  Genome      Helix        // Species "own" this
//Methods
  Expire(Extinct) {...}    // Saddest LifeSim event
  Compete(SPACE) {...}     // Space invaders!
  React(Evolve) {...}    } // Survival of the fittest
```

Species own the genome, a repository of information.

A species is a "living" thing in that it "wants" to survive and prosper. A species will React() to changes in the environment, not in a moment like a critter but over millennia. Like any living thing a species competes, but for SPACE rather than food because it doesn't Eat(). The species prospers by increasing its range, either by outcompeting other species or evolving more successful DNA to inhabit tougher environments. A species is a complex adaptive system that uses DNA[85] to do the adapting.

Species are a phenomenon of information

A species is a *phenomenon* of life, not a living critter itself, but a kind of living, adapting, evolving

[85] Or RNA for micros or something simpler for the Replicator (expired)

"thing."[86] Life rests on a tripod of matter, energy, and information. Living critters are composed of matter, but species are not. Nor it easy to pinpoint any energy specifically expended by the species. Therefore, the species is purely a phenomenon of INFORMATION. Physical DNA atoms (of MATTER) are the transmission vector, but the *arrangement* of those atoms belongs to the species. In the parlance of object-oriented (Java-like) programming, the species "owns" the gene pool, here stored in helical format. The species evolves by recombining its DNA and following the winners. The Meaning of Life for a species is to evolve. It does that by remembering successful combinations of DNA. Genetic losers are lost forever. (Memes can remember both success and failure, as in Og's failure to survive whatever it was).

Subdivisions of species

Species can have sub-groups of identifiably different but still interfertile individuals. If human husbandry has caused genetic separations, we call them *Breeds*. Different environments cause noticeable differences. If genetically separated from the rest of the species for sufficient time, the sub-groups might

---

[86] Most Java objects are physical things, not vaporous phenomena.

diverge into new species. Wide-ranging humans have natural *Ethnicities* with minor, but recognizable, genetic distinctions as well as tribal/cultural separations. The largest of the "natural" human divisions is the *People*, the most successful of which have their own *Country*. Less successful ethnicities are minorities within another people's country.

Characteristics of Mobs

A social species has subgroups because the species has too many individual critters to fit in one place. The passenger pigeon was an exception, with all of them in one humungous flock. That didn't work out too well. *Mob* is the collective term for any of the "named" communal forms of social animals on Earth. This includes herds, schools, packs, gaggles, and many cuter names. Mobs are collections of critters (of one species, ignoring commensals) separated by distance or borders from other mobs. A *Swarm* is a temporary group, but herds and such are "permanent" subsets of the species. There is generally only one *type* of Mob per species, though nurturing, social critters have a mob and family, at least while the pups are in the nest. So, a mare can have a *herd* and a *family* and might have divided loyalties at times.

Why Mobs work

Mobs use "mass quantities" to help their members survive. Herds stampede, which works because you can avoid one but not the whole mass. Fish schools and zebra herds Defend(Dazzle) to confuse. Offensively, at least some members of the *Pack* get to bite from behind. Critters gather into a mob for a reason. The best reason to call a huddle is to avoid becoming lunch. That applies to all species except top predators. The second-best reason to mass the troops is to *obtain* lunch. All predatory social critters prefer this to dining alone.

Generic Mob and its Members

```
class Mob extends Group     { // Stick with us!
//Attribute    Data Type      Comment
  Species      String        {// Mobs are exclusive
  Members      List[Brainiac]
  Alpha        Member         // Pack leader (optional)
//Methods
  Submit( ) {...}             // default: Follow
  Expire(Disband) {...} // Another kind of death
  Deny(Membership) {...}
  Sentry( ) {...}             // Many eyes
  Defend( ) {...}        }    // For flank defense
```

The advantages of mobbing

Mobs are groups of critters of the same species that gather because it benefits the individual critters. *Not being alone* gives the critter several advantages. It is good for offense or defense and for gathering intel on the enemy. The mob relies on an instinctive drive to form a huddle. The bond between critters and their mob gives the mob some measure of control over the paths its critters make through life. The mob "controls" its critters movements, though the method of control (who's in charge?) might be vague. The mob doesn't control many other aspects of its critters' lives, since most of their lives consists of moving and eating[87] and eating is an individual critter's job. Some mobs might deny membership to a potential new member,[88] but seldom eject an existing member. *Tribes* will eject a member when that member behaves badly. One huge advantage the individual obtains in a mob is extra eyes to spot danger. Warm critters can hear a warning chirp from the eyeballing mob member. (This isn't available to schools.) Lots of mobs Defend() the cubs. Few Mobs defend their members as explicitly as the Yak. Defend(Circle). Other kinds of mob offer no help at

---

[87] A cow doesn't have a life; it has lunch.

[88] Prey herds are generally more liberal than predator packs in accepting a stranger.

all. The mob works more for the species than the individual. Species are totally heartless in their attitudes regarding the survival of individuals. A yak circle is an *emergent* defensive behavior. It might be responsible for all the surviving yak in the world, if the yak herd that invented it Prospered() enough. If there are (still) yak herds that don't form defensive circles, then this behavior is not instinctive. The yak circle might be a bovine meme! Yak are members of a herd, so also have the stampede in their arsenal of group-related survival tricks. Schools and flocks don't get this super-power.

Specific mob subclasses methods

```
class School extends Mob {
  Defend(Dazzle) {...}      }     // Shiny defense
class Herd extends Mob      {
  Move(Stampede) {...}      }[89]
class Yak extends Species   {
  Defend(Circle) {...}      }     // Horns out!
```

Predator Mobs (Packs)

Social predators get to defend the *Pack* but can't stampede. Predators attack together because

[89] When four hooves just won't do

it gives them the advantage of encirclement. We won't say they "Swarm() the prey" because we're using swarm as a class. There's nothing illegal in Java about declaring a *class* and a *method()* with the same name, but it's stupid. The advantage that packs have is that they can attack from all directions, something a single animal can't do. That's why they are packing.

```
class Pack extends Mob     {
  Move(Encircle) {...}     }   // Predator tactics
```

Volunteers – Members of the Mob

Critters join a herd voluntarily, or they are born into one and don't leave. They can choose to leave or submit to the will of the mob.

```
class Member extends Brainiac {
//Attribute   Data Type      Comment
  Rank        int            // Social status in the mob
  Duties      List[String]   // Tribal contract
//Methods
  Submit(Behave) {...}       //More than just Follow!
  Choose(Maverick) {...} }   // Quit the mob
class Elder extends Member {
  Teach( ) {...} }           //Tribes only
class Youth extends Member {
```

Mature(Learn){...} }   // If they listen

Mobs are composed of individual critters, called Members of the mob or tribe. Active participation in a mob or tribe is voluntary. Any herd can have a maverick. As mentioned above, going solo might be hazardous to your health. All the member needs to do is follow the mob, the default duty of all mob members. Within the mobs of most species Members have genetically inspired Sentry() duties. Some have Defend() duties on their list. Enforcement of the contract for a *prey* mob is effectively provided by the teeth of its predators. Additionally, some mobs enforce behaviors *internally*, as in Alpha.Dominate() or Hen.Peck(). Rank within the mob determines who gives and who takes. These are instinctive behaviors in some mobs (and therefore all tribes). Additionally, tribes have culturally derived behaviors (memes) on how they expect the individual to behave. Following the tribe's rules is just as voluntary as joining a tribe, but you risk Mob.Reject() if you behave too badly. This includes a tribe with a license to kill (Army, Country, sometimes Church) ejecting a member from this life! After the death penalty, the most serious outcome of tribal justice in the Stone Age was to get kicked out of the band. That was close to fatal.

Characteristics of Tribes

Tribes are mobs with a culture. A few animal mobs have a "culture," which means they employ methods() that other mobs of that species don't. These behaviors usually involve food. Mobs, even adjacent mobs of the same species, might specialize in different kinds of food. That sort of thing can lead to new species. The distinction between tribe and mob can be blurry in the animal kingdom. If an old elephant leads the herd to a "forgotten" water-hole, and that happens again fifty years later, is that culture? Is a flock's migration route chosen by old geese? But ignoring family, other species have only one *kind* of mob. Man has several different tribes. These tribes cover many more activities than "directing" its critters where to go. That's the mob's job. People have more interesting and varied methods than cows, so tribes have more controls to tweak. If they control every aspect of your life, you're in the wrong tribe.

Tribes have the characteristics of Mobs plus:

1. Tribes have a cultural (non-genetic) memory storage process. It preserves INFORMATION critical to the survival and prosperity of the tribe. Memory allows the tribe to evolve, a trait they share with

species but not mobs. Mobs never get any better at mobbing.

2. Tribes need a justice system. Interacting tribal members often butt heads. The tribe's justice system must resolve disputes fairly or members will seek a new tribe. The default behavior for individual critters in conflict is Critter.Duel(). Some mobs use Alpha.Dominate() or Hen.Peck() to disincentivize bad behavior. Humans expect our tribes to be more sophisticated than these "primitive" behaviors, except in the family where Mom.Rules().

3. Tribes have a social contract wherein they expect their members to behave in certain ways to earn the benefits of membership. This goes beyond the mob rule, "Stick together!" Members have *duties*. You agree to show up at work on time and work all day to receive a stipend to keep you fed. Your duty is also to do your best or be a slacker and nobody likes a slacker.

4. Human Tribes come in three basic strengths. At the top are Family and Country, the two tribes you might die for.

Next are *Institutions*, which have less power but more than *Communities*.

Class: Tribe

LifeSim describes Tribe as a child of the Mob class. Both are composed of brainy, social critters of the same species. We measure with two attributes the depth and quality of the commitment of the tribe's members to the success and prosperity of the tribe. The willingness of a member to die for the Tribe is the maximal commitment. It is normally only available to Family and Country, declared below with ToDieFor=True. We rate Morale within the tribe with a five-bin list ranging from Saint to Slacker. The success of a tribe is tied directly to its members' willingness to sacrifice for the cause, but it's mostly their TIME that's sacrificed, not their lives. Another measure of success, more relevant to Tribe. Prosper() than Tribe.Survive(), is the Status attribute. This measures how well your tribe is doing compared to others of the same class.

```
class Tribe extends Mob {  // Cultured mob
//Attribute   Data Type    Comment
  Purpose     String=""    // Why this tribe exists
  ToDieFor    Boolean      // Depth of commitment
  Members List[Warm]       // Not just humans
```

```
  Elders     List[Elder]// Teaching Members
  Culture    List[Meme]// Local behaviors
  Morale     5Bin          // Members' attitude
  Status     5Bin          // Tribal success[90]
//Methods
  Evolve(RefineMemes ) {...}
  Arbitrate( ){...} }   // in lieu of Compete(Duel)
```

Optional attribute for Class success

For the class itself (not the instances), we might add a Five Bin attribute for tracking the relative influence of the various *classes* of Tribe in our lives. A Trending attribute could rate a *Class* as increasing or decreasing in "power." The class Kingdom has been trending down since the Age of Plenty. Empires are down but hardly out. The hunter-gatherer life-style is way down but if civilization collapses, the Band will get back together. Family became more important with farming but has taken hits recently. Bureau.Trending = "Way Up".

Tribal capabilities

The primary method that invokes culture is Tribe.Teach(). Natural tribes teach manners (how

---

[90] Varies from Prosperous to Failing

to behave) through memes and a few techno-memes like starting a fire. Modern tribes teach SOPs. A tribe must manage internal conflict in a way that members perceive as fair. A tribe needs a justice system to arbitrate the inevitable disputes between its members. To fail at this – for the members to perceive injustice–is the best way for a tribe to die. A failure in the tribe's Arbitrate() method is one cause of low Morale and Status = "Failing" or even Extant=False. One class of tribe, the Country, claims the judicial right to end your life as a result of arbitration. At a minimum, a tribe can exclude a potential member or eject a misbehaving existing member. A tribe justifies its existence when it contributes to its members' survival and prosperity. Tribes promise their members some form(s) of service and members must pay for that service. Members mostly pay with their time, working for tribal purposes instead of themselves. The tribe also demands you behave according to its memes. To submit or not to submit, that is the question. Tribes that cannot inspire their members to submit are in trouble. This goes back to a failure in the Mob.Bond() method.

Tribal duties

You choose to enhance your tribes unless you're a jerk. For most of us, the best way to improve the world is through our family tribe, by raising better children. Your odds of doing that *genetically* are one in four.[91] You have more control over the culture you Bequeath() your kids. Responsible parents improve the odds of their children surviving and prospering with good memes. You can improve the survival and prosperity of your other tribes by refining their SOPs. It's not too hard to leave the world a better place for having endured your existence. You are born with an instinctive tendency to support your tribes, family most of all. Your predisposition to help can range from selfish to selfless in the standard game of genetic roulette. The selfish either don't want to help or they don't even think of helping. Selfishness is just one of many human characteristics that follow a normal distribution through genetics. Basic competence in getting the job done ranges from Hopeless and Klutzy to Handy and Elite. Other normal human characteristics (not binned here) include friendliness or curiosity or cruelty or piety. We should be accustomed to dealing with the crazies at either end of these distributions by now, but some of them are really annoying. These characteristics can translate to whole tribes if reinforced by the appropriate meme. Selfishness may be the human characteristic that, through the Social

[91] Normal distribution ("stepped" bell curve) for a sample size of 4 = 1 superior, 2 average, 1 inferior

Contract, most directly impacts the success of the Tribe. Selfish memes are therefore, with respect to the survival and prosperity of the tribe, the worst memes of all.

Tribal Specs

There are three main groups of critters on Earth: mobs, tribes, and species. Genetic information ties Species together and holds Mobs together with social instincts. Tribes are distinguished by their brains, not their genes. These are two *very* different systems of information storage. DNA is chemical. Brains are electric.

Tribes are cultured

Mobs seldom get better at mobbing.

Mobs include herds and schools and flocks of critters, who mostly gather for protection. Defend(Confuse) is the default. It works to distract predators on land, sea, and air. But Mobs seldom get better at confusing the foe. Mobs have no memory, no culture, and no evolution. Tribes have a means of transmitting knowledge to new members. Herds can last centuries but don't get any better at it. Tribes get better at doing whatever it is they do.

Tribes have a memory. Pass it on.

A Tribe is a collection of critters with an institutional memory. A few animal troops/pods/herds have a distinct culture. They have techniques that others of their species lack. In the nature versus nurture debate, nurture kicks in with Mom, the first teacher. Other tribes have Elders. Tribe.Teach() is a method unavailable to mobs. Tribal memory by itself does not cause evolution. That comes from transferring the memories by meme to the replenishment units, who improve them.

Culture's Goal: tribal survival (Prosperity is nice, too.)

Cultural information contains tools and techniques for the survival and prosperity of the tribe. A society's songs and dance, or food and dress, do much to distinguish one culture from another. However, they seldom contribute directly to tribal survival.[92] Genetic heritage can distinguish one culture from another but offers few competitive advantages. The Japanese will survive and prosper without basketball trophies.[93]

---

[92] Eskimo furs and Vietnamese monsoon hats excepted.

[93] And white men can't jump.

A distinctive culture distinguishes a Tribe from a Mob.

A culture is the sum of the non-instinctive behaviors of a tribe. Genetic behaviors apply to all groups of that species. Culture distinguishes one group from another *within that species* due to a significant difference in behavior. A certain pod of orcas creates a bow wave to sweep seals off small ice floes. As the only pod known to do that, they have a "culture".[94] That pod now has two methods of transmitting information, DNA and brains. Discovering how rapidly new techniques spread to other groups of that species is probably worth a (very long-term) grant. Human memes are vocal and fast movers compared to the memes of animals that don't use language.

Culture transmits learned behaviors

Grandma starts a family tradition.

Cultures come from learned behaviors. Animals learn by watching. The calves watch Mom and learn some of her tricks. Most of her tricks are instinctive, but some just might come from Grandma. All nurturing (warm) species, avian or mammalian,

[94] We should call them a *tribe* of whales.

improve the odds of survival of their young by feeding and protecting them. Some parents play with the kids, sharpening the skills that will help them survive. Mom doesn't need to be "actively" teaching for her experiences to be passed down to the next generation. The pups just watch what Mom does and copy it. If Grandma had a new trick and this got as far as the grandcubs, she started a family tradition. Tradition is a form of institutional knowledge, so family qualifies as a tribe. Family, usually just Mom, is the oldest class of tribe.

Focus on human behavior vs environment or other humans

Our focus is on human *behavior*, on how humans interact with each other and secondarily, other parts of the environment like other critters and non-living matter. We have different memes (suggesting different behaviors) for members of the tribe (We) and non-members (They). Our *processes* cover the non-human parts of the environment. Processes store knowledge of how to start a fire or shear a sheep. *Process* memes (techno-memes) are highly mobile and accepted quickly across multiple societies. The Money meme has proven highly contagious. *Behavioral* memes like the Barbarian or Trust memes travel less readily.

Other Tribal Facts

Tribes are immortal but can go extinct.

The knowledge of the elders can "outlive" the teacher, so tribes are effectively immortal. Still, tribes "wish" to survive and prosper, just like a real critter. The reason tribes work is they help their members survive and prosper. A prosperous tribe can "live" (remain extant) longer than any member. They can go extinct, of course. The old gods could be killed even though they were "immortal." Tribes "want" to survive, even if the justification for their existence vanishes. They can hang on long past their expiration date.

Tribes aren't real.

Tribes can't really "wish" (to survive and prosper) because they are not "real" in the physical sense. A tribe has no mass and occupies no space. Tribes are an *agreement* among individual critters to act together for their survival and prosperity. They are a *phenomenon* of social life, with no substance but substantial impact. Tribes don't wish or think or feel. It is, however, convenient to think of Uncle Sam as alive when he needs you.

Tribes are Voluntary.

People join tribes voluntarily. They submit to the rules of the tribe to obtain the benefits of membership in the tribe. So do the members of mobs. This is the *Social Contract*. It applies to all social animals living in herds or schools or flocks. The rule of the mob for prey animals is, "Stick together or get eaten!" This works for all but the top predators as well. For predators, it's "Stick together or go hungry!" Individual critters have instincts that encourage joining and staying with the group. However, critters control their own movements and can always go maverick (or loco, if their mental model breaks). Suppressing the herding instinct is difficult, but it's legal to go solo for any critter smart enough to make a choice. That's basically anything with a brain, approximately since sharks emerged.

Tribes have a boundary, forming a We and a They.

There are memes for how we treat members of our own tribe and for how we treat outsiders. A tribe's attitude toward *Others* is one of the first things a visiting outsider wants to know. How easily your tribe adopts the memes of foreigners reflects your tribe's *agility*, an important survival characteristic in a dynamic, competitive environment. The We/They border applies to every member in every tribe. All tribes expect members to prefer We over They. Neutrality is for high-end Liberals on the Xeno axis.

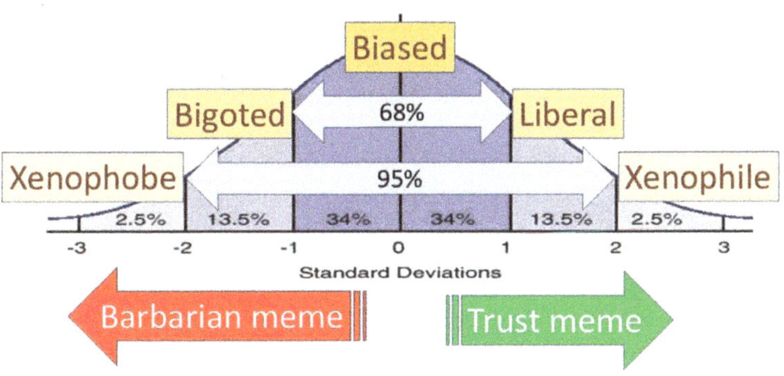

Five-Bin Xeno Distribution

This is the only Five-Bin chart where the central 68% is *not* labelled "Normal". A bias of We over They is normal. If you don't prefer your friends over strangers, you're not a very good friend. The Xeno axis shows five degrees of attitude (bins) a member of a tribe might have for non-members. In addition to the attitudes of individuals, we might dump tribes into one of these five bins. This, and other, Five-Bin charts have 68% of the population behaving normally...it's a Normal distribution, after all. 95% of the population is *sane*. The outer 5%, 2.5% either side, are nuts. The two bins between one and two standard deviations out harbor people with slightly odd, but not quite crazy attitudes.

Equality is crazy.

The Xeno axis represents one dimension of liberality, based on tolerance of Others. The "classical liberal" has a more expansive definition which includes freedom-loving and pro-capitalism attitudes. Those belong on their own *axes* of social merit. The Barbarian meme tended toward xenophobia. We've been nicer to our neighbors since the Trust meme caught on. It's still normal to be biased toward your own. If you think we should treat Others equally with members of our own Tribe, you are beyond Liberal. The cut line for exact equality lies between Liberal and Xenophile. If you want true equality, you're borderline crazy.

How to sense Them: By ear

There are a variety of signals that can distinguish We from They. By ear, language has always been a firm indicator. An accent might indicate a new member of the tribe. You would more likely assume they are a part of We in a cosmopolitan society than an isolated one.

On purpose

Dress and coiffure and gestures can broadcast tribal colors when They *want* to be known as Them. Street gangs do it every day. Lederhosen only come out once a year, as a behavior within *communities* of German origin. This is a bonding rite (strictly We). Gang colors are We vs They. Biker clothing deliberately invokes aspects of the Barbarian meme.

Inherent ID

Ethnic distinctions can serve as visual signals, race being the most obvious. Presumably, neighboring Stone Age peoples were of the same race, and discerned We from They by language or gang colors. With the relative ease of transport in the Age of Empire, visible differences between far-flung peoples became obvious. So, they invented the Races of Man, a model not supported by later analysis. The human "race" is a *Species* named Homo Sapiens by the followers of (Sage) Carl Linnaeus or Homo Sapiens Sapiens by stutterers. The human species has very wide natural variation because it ranges across so many environments. Most other species are very local, and their critters like upon one another. Humans have ranged widely enough to be obviously different without depending on language or dress. Interactions between obviously far-flung peoples became more frequent in the Age of Empire and common in the Age of Plenty.

Race

Skin color primarily indicates the length of time that a given gene line has lived far away from the equator. Other distinctive racial characteristics result from long periods of isolation from other gene lines. By this measure, Australian aborigines deserve to be a race of their own. Skin color has nothing to do with the pudginess of Eskimos, but the cause is the same. Being so far from the equator, they evolved to conserve heat. The Watusi grew tall for the opposite reason. The epicanthic fold, whatever the cause, was apparently distinct enough to justify the Mongoloid label to (at the time) about half of humanity. The reason for the difference doesn't matter. The minimum requirement is that We can tell They from a distance. Visibly larger noses suggest genes fine-tuned for the desert. That was enough for cold-nosed Europeans to recognize Jews. Antisemitism and racism are forms of ethnic intolerance, but ethnicism isn't a popular word, so we misuse ”racism”. Visual differences are enough to trigger bigotry if the memes trend that way. We can track the progress of a People or a Civilization with the Liberal meme. A liberal society ignores visible differences, legally and intellectually if not emotionally. Emotions are harder for memes to conquer. Visibly different people are going to trigger an instinctive Stranger/Danger reaction. Civilized memes can tamp down that reaction to something less than a full combat posture.

The rise of liberalism

Liberal societies tolerate minor cultural divergences. They can question morally and ban legally major differences without being bigoted. A sovereign people can always say to a stranger, “You can’t do that here!” This is legal and moral discrimination (valid ethnicism) based on the *behavior* of the Other. Racism is immoral discrimination based on *visual* differences. Ethnic intolerance in general does not need a visual trigger. Religious intolerance has its own scorecard. It can be based on people who look alike and behave alike but do not think alike. In the West, religious tolerance memes emerged in the American colonies. Northern Ireland took a while.

Religion

The modern liberal meme may have begun with acceptance of an invisible distinction–religion. Practitioners of a different faith are not ordinarily distinguishable by sight but might be by their behavior. Religions are an effective place to store behavioral memes. In tribal terms, religions *exist* to get people to behave. The Jews had ten or fifteen[95] rules for proper behavior. Preachers have been chastising bad behavior for a long time. Religious tolerance is a behavior of the West, a spinoff of the Trust meme, perhaps. A related liberal trend has been that strangers have not just been tolerated, but increasingly welcomed to join the We. A few societies actively recruit new members from afar. This has worked better in some societies than others. The key to success is assimilation, when recent arrivals adopt the behavioral memes of their new homeland. They can keep some of their process memes, especially ethnic food.

---

95 with Mel Brooks as Moses

Tribal Emergence

Tribes Emerge when needed.

A new class of Tribe will *emerge* when humans need to gather for a new purpose. This is quite rare. The Army was the first artificial Tribe. The TV Evangelical tribe is one of the newest. A new *instance* of a standard class of tribe will emerge when the same old problems pop up. A new *Band* will emerge if you dump some survivors on an island. If two tribes form, you get a reality show. Gathering energy is the original purpose of the aptly named hunter-gatherer band. Bonding in a group/Mob to gather energy goes back to our primate days. Back then, we gathered in troops, an omnivorous sort of mob. We graduated to tribe, by these definitions, before we could talk, since many survival lessons can be taught just by gesture. Perhaps troops of monkeys that teach their kids how to crack nuts should be promoted to Bands of monkeys when they demonstrate the basic cultural method, Tribe.Teach().

New purposes for gathering post-Stone Age

New *forms* (classes) of Tribe emerge when new purposes evolve. The People was the largest kind of tribe of the Stone Age. It emerged when we started talking. Language creates a natural We/They boundary so, in a sense, language created the *Homeland*. Prior to that, the largest collection of humanoid critters was the *Band*, which has a *Territory*. After that, and long before Barbarians emerged, the *People* were the standard unit for defending the homeland. They met irregularly, and didn't establish a tribe for war. That came with the Ag meme.

The first "artificial" Tribe

The Army emerged when it became necessary to steal food from farmers properly. Other classes of tribe have emerged as the need arose. *Kingdoms* formed when Barbarians or emperors forced a Stone Age or early Ag Age people to reorganize or die. An *Aristocracy* followed. The *Corporation* as a tribal form emerged at the beginning of the Age of Plenty. They replaced the *Guilds*, which had inferior memes. *Unions* emerged to compensate for some corporate flaws. *Universities* emerged to spread laic knowledge. *Advocacies* formed when we got rich and bored, to support all sorts of purposes. The chart below lists some of the kinds of Tribe humanity has invented, and the reason for it.

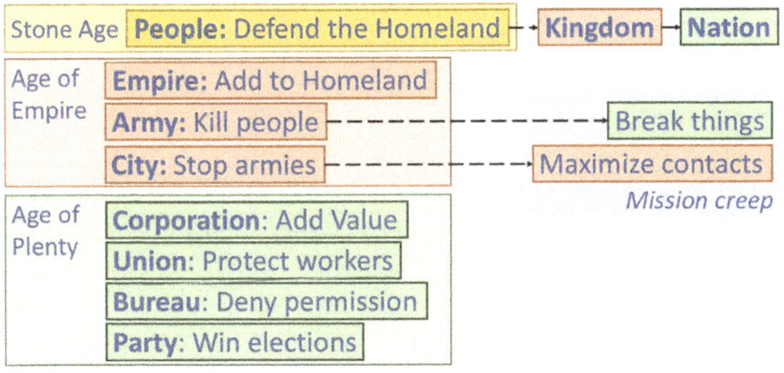
Tribal Missions
Stone Age
People: Defend the Homeland
Kingdom
Nation
Age of Empire
Empire: Add to Homeland
Army: Kill people
Break things
City: Stop armies
Maximize contacts
Mission creep
Age of Plenty
Corporation: Add Value
Union: Protect workers
Bureau: Deny permission
Party: Win elections

New Purposes, new Tribes

This chart leaves out the oldest Tribes. *Family* exists for the purpose of raising (nurturing) survivable replacements for the parents. The Stone Age *Band* exists to gather energy. (The band will defend its territory, but that's not *why* hominids gather into bands.) The standard homeland defense organization is people-sized. It was rather unorganized in the Stone Age, with War Chief being a temporary title. That responsibility shifted to Kings and Nations over the years. Empires do not just defend the homeland, but vigorously try to add to it. The purpose of the army is now to kill people and break things, but the property destruction part came after we got rich. Early armies killed people and *took* things. The city tribe was invented for its walls but became more important as a place to meet and greet and get things done. It is said that corporations exist to make money, but that's just the scoring system. Its real purpose is to combine MATTER, ENERGY, and INFORMATION in ways that are more valuable than before. Unions emerged because of corporate tribal behaviors. Bureaucracies were invented to stop people from doing what they wanted, for the good of the people, of course. Political parties are an Age of Plenty Tribe, as are museums and charities and the Press. They all exist for different purposes.

Death throes for Class: Tribe

The purpose that drove the creation of the tribe is not guaranteed to remain applicable forever, but every instance that class of tribe will try to Survive() anyway. The city began as a homeland defense tribe but stayed on as an Agent of Chaos (an evolution accelerator). The Press once sold valuable, timely information on the status of the System of the World. They now sell entertainment. The introduction of the Internet did that. A change in the environment can affect a whole class of tribe and all its instances.

Rejecting instances of the Class

An individual instance of any tribe can stray from its purpose if it gets corrupted by other memes. When this happens, its members need to ask themselves if their home tribe still has value. If it doesn't, they might hop to a different local tribe. This is commonly expressed by getting a new job. That can lead to the death of an individual tribe but not the whole class. The Whigs are gone but political parties still work. Entire classes of tribe seldom go completely out of style, but the Band and Guild are almost obsolete, and the Kingdom isn't what it used to be.

Corrupted institutions

Multiple instances of the tribe can go corrupt together while others remain true to their purpose. We can attribute this to a conspiracy but is more likely a standard tribal battle. In the case of Academia in America over the last sixty years, the Marxist community has spread its memes, trying to replace traditional academic memes with its own. Its adherents do not need to conspire. Their memes hold them together.

Cooperating Tribes

Intertribal cooperation can be beneficial for some tribes, though always at the cost of others. There's just so much loyalty to go around. Church plus country form a theocracy, which suppresses all other forms of tribe. Other collaborations are less explicitly confrontational. In fact, it can be hard to find a specific tribe to blame when they're all in on it. Consider the Go West meme as a nation-building exercise. The Go West meme was named for a member of the press, but all sorts of tribes were in favor of breaking up the extended family to get those lazy uncles to work harder. The bankers wanted to make loans for the new houses they'd need. The manufacturers wanted to fill them up with carpets and such. The military wanted more carpet factories, which they could turn to tank production when the Nazis came again. It is a very effective way to build the strength of a nation. The uncles get mortgages and need to work harder because desperation is such a fine incentive. Many tribes prosper from the Go West meme, breaking up the extended family to make the separate individuals work harder. Hollywood laugh-tracks have extended the meme to "Go West, young woman." Their snide slurs about "still living in the parent's basement" are now gender neutral. Hollywood and other tribes benefit from the

Go West meme. It's hard to call it a conspiracy when so many important institutions are on the same page. They don't need to communicate, much less communicate secretly. They don't need to conspire, in the legal sense, to support the meme.

Paperwork

Human Tribes come in different strengths.

The important tribal forms in history include empires and kingdoms, armies, corporations, and bureaucracies. Less important tribes range from universities and other "institutions" to less formal "communities" like bowling leagues. Only the Country has the power of life and death over its members (legally). Others have less power but can still sting. A weak tribe can only shun or chide you.

Your tribal budget

You belong to several tribes. Most of us have a family and country, the top tier tribes. You might belong to a church. Unless you are self-employed, you have a corporation. (A Mom & Pop is still a corporation and a tiny, stand-alone tribe.) You can join a club or advocacy. All require some of your time. Some will take a check, which also means your time, basically. Your whole day is either Me Time or Tribal Time. You need a budget.

The Territorial Tribes of Man

Lots of Tribes

Man has more kinds of groups than any other critter. All critters, down to microbes, have a species. Social critters (animals only and not all of them) have a mob. Some have a Mom, the oldest teacher and first tribal critter. Cultured monkeys and orcas have two tribes while they are young. Then Mom pretty much disappears as an influencer. Human moms stick around forever, so we have Family our whole lives. We also have a special tribe called a People, which other critters don't have because they don't talk. Since the Stone Age, we have separated ourselves from other peoples by language. There have been many mergers and migrations since then, but a distinct language is still the best border around a people. In addition to man's "natural" tribes, we have created new kinds of Tribes. The formal ones we call *Institutions*. Less formal are the *Communities* we form. They all exist because they serve a purpose that improves our lives. We territorial critters defend the land that feeds us. We have tried several organizational forms to defend the land since the

Stone Age. We are territorial on several levels. While that is hardly the most important task for the family, homestead defense is a fallback position.

The smallest Territorial Tribe: Street gangs

The smallest turf-holding tribes are smaller than stone age bands. The urban environment might have something to do with that. Street gangs have a crude structure and rudimentary memory retention. The justice system is little more evolved than the Whim of the Alpha. Street gangs don't morph into adult criminal gangs, but their members may switch tribes on adulthood. They have had little impact on the course of human history, on a par with (adult) urban Neighborhoods, which have not been responsible for territorial defense since the days of hamlets. Neighborhoods share the same turf as street gangs, but the two are very separate tribes. Neither are very important classes of tribe in terms of their impact on history. Street gangs do demonstrate the spontaneous *emergence* of a Tribe within a population that has no other means of common defense. They also demonstrate a high replenishment rate. Street gangs are primarily a teenage phenomenon. They change generations, swapping out the entire membership, perhaps twice as fast as Family (the standard). Boy Scouts troops replenish their junior members faster, but the scoutmasters (Elders) carry on the tribal traditions. The Elders in street gangs have little more experience than the newest members.

Criminal gangs

A criminal gang with a territory defends it with their lives. They are closer in size, structure, and purpose to a stone age band than any other modern tribe. The Mafia emerged as a super tribe (cartel) to coordinate the market. It developed a unique meme called Omerta, famous despite being a behavior very local to this odd kind of tribe. Criminal cartels can have considerable impact on "weak" societies. Clans, kingdoms, and empires (barbarians at heart) can all fall for klepto memes. Nations oppose them most effectively (perhaps), but it's a constant struggle.

Family, the Oldest Tribe

In praise of Mom

The *Family* consists of Mom and the kits/pups/calves/chicklets. Most of the animal world does not require a Dad. Mom stays with and protects the pups. Sea turtles are terrible moms. Moms also feed the cubs. Crocodile moms do the protection part, but for dinner, the chicks are on their own.

Family code

```
class Family extends Tribe {
 {set Purpose ='Raise viable replacements'
  set ToDieFor = True
  set Culture[1]96  = "Mom rules!"}
//Attribute   Data Type    Comment
 Mom          Elder        // Warm (at least)
 Dad          Boolean      // Optional
 Surname      String       // Human only
 Privilege    Boolean      // For aristocrats
//Methods
 Protect( ) {...}          // Nurturing #1
 Feed( ) {...}             // Nurturing #2 97
 Bequeath( ) {...}         // Human only
 AddValue( ) {...} }       // Post Ag "Business" 98
```

Why motherhood works

Birds and mammals provide their young the nurturing services of protection and feeding. The class Tribe covers teaching, the third advantage of nurturing. When a cat mom brings a mouse home

---

[96] Only a geek uses 0 as the first index of a list

[97] Nurturing #3 is Elder.Teach(). Mom is the original teacher.

[98] The *Family* owns this method, which represents the intellectual property of traders, farmers, and herders. The *Band* owns hunting methods.

for the kits to play with, that's deliberate teaching. But the young can just learn by watching Mom going about her everyday business. The tribal arbitration method of the family is Mom.Rules(). If she has a special behavior that helps her and her young survive and prosper, she starts a family tradition. Nurturing ends when the cubs go off on their own, but the family traditions remain if the kittens remember. Technically, the proof of success that a tradition has started takes a generation, so praise Grandma, too. If Grandma's behaviors include eating different foods, family traditions may lead to new species. For humans, the ability to talk enhances the ability to teach, so we nurture more than the average bear. The lifetime commitment of a human family is much longer than most species. Human families are the tribe that invented inheritance. Animal families don't have that many possessions so don't need this method. The special Bequeath(Crown) parameter applies to certain families in kingdoms and empires. (Those same families are members of the *Aristocracy*, which is an international *community*, not a territorial defense Tribe.)

Band, the Natural Tribe

Hunting and gathering for fun and profit

The hunter-gatherer *Troop* (child of Mob, not Tribe) is the natural group for all simians and all but one primate[99]. The group performs the collective defense function against predators and, for territorial critters, to repel invaders. Troops are one category of vegetarian or omnivorous critters. The carnivorous version is the Pack. The troop or pack is the tightest tribe after the family. Your ancestors from way back depended on this small group of critters for their very lives and their help in the eternal quest for Energy. There was no larger Tribe for the territorial defense function until we started to talk.

Troops evolve to bands

Tool making has emerged several times in simian or primate history. The knowledge would have spread outside the family for every primate but the aye-aye, which doesn't have a larger social structure. The band has Elders, inherited from class Tribe, who become the keeper of the Lore. The human band

[99] The adult aye-aye is a Loner.

also has a Chief, the first titled member, although many troops have an Alpha.

Band class

```
class Band extends Tribe    {// aka Merry Band
 {set Purpose='Obtain energy'} // Together!
//Attribute     Data Type     Comment
  Chief         Member        // Established leader
//Methods
  Remember(Tools) {...}       // Early tech
  Hunt(Together)              //More tricks than Packs
  Gather(Safely)              // Don't eat that![100]
```

Tool focused bands

The elders in nut hammering troops of monkeys spread techno-memes by demonstration. They use *found* objects like rocks or sticks. Chimps take the next step and refine their tools, trimming their poking sticks to catch termites better, for instance. Several species, Neanderthal and Denisovan for sure, have combined *multiple* elements of the environment into more useful objects. They emerged from their Stick Age to their Stone Age (short for Stick+Stone+Vine Age). The elders transmit tool

[100] Elders warn of poison berries and yellow snow

memes to help the band survive and prosper. Any member of the band can improve a techno meme and share the new knowledge. The band is tight in that respect. The band "owns" that memory.

The natural age

Hominids have evolved within the band/troop for 5 million years. *Humanoids* in this model emerged 500,00 years ago. We assume they were all territorial. When one band met another band, conflict might have ensued. More commonly, the side with the bigger numbers got to hunt there that day. Some hominid species might have used Sticks. That didn't change the nature of conflict. It was still band on band, not what we now call war. Language did that. Late-stage humanoid species might have talked and warred people on people. Humanoids evolved beyond the club (a found object) to the sharpened stick, an early product of the Reshape(MATTER) method. That method led to clothing and out of Africa. The Stone Age for Homo Sapiens (as a late-stage humanoid) began 50,000 years ago. The Band was the dominant social form until the Ag meme (and a bit beyond. The Hamlet is basically a band.)

Modern equivalents

Outside the family, Stone Age bands were the tightest social organizations humans have ever known. Not many modern jobs require this level of commitment. The closest may be the platoon on land, ship's crew at sea, or a criminal gang. These are among the few modern tribes where the members depend on each other for their very lives. For most of us there are no tribes in our lives, apart from the family, as tight as the old Band. This doesn't necessarily mean we should get the band back together.

People, the Human Tribe

Levels of organization

No animal except Man has more than two tribes (or mobs). All simians live in a family within a troop or band. A People is a (somewhat unified) group of bands and represents a third layer of tribalhood. The bonds between bands were relatively weak in the Stone Age. It strengthened when barbarians emerged. The bonds within some peoples were strengthened in the late Stone Age with the Monument meme. Any group project (like war) builds bonds.

The Peoples of the world

```
class People extends Tribe {// We should talk!
  {set Purpose='Defend territory and culture'}
//Attribute    Data Type    Comment
  Territory    Area         //"Informal" Homeland
//Methods
  Defend(Territory) {...}
  Remember(Lore) {...}   }  // Stories and memes
```

Standard evolutionary path of a People

The bonds that hold a people together grow stronger on the *Main Sequence* of societal progression. A loosely bonded Stone Age people would develop their versions of the kingdom and/or empire tribal forms, and perhaps emerge as a modern nation state. At each stage, the people bonded more closely. Stone Age peoples were bonded by language, bits of lore, and a fairly uniform set of memes for surviving in the wild. We share a wider variety of memes since the days when hunter and gatherer were the only jobs available. A People that survived the Stone Age had to be adaptable. They had to learn to work together in new ways, which means new kinds of tribes and a lot of new memes. The People remain the most important *We* in terms of surviving bad behavior by *Them*. Surviving the bad behavior of its own bad actors is a function of the justice system of any tribe.

Drought driven togetherness

The best reason for Stone Age bands to work together was a drought. The structure that the bands "formed" for this purpose was more of a *Swarm*, without the immortality of a Mob or the culture of a Tribe. The Stone Age didn't have armies. They had swarms. That does not mean there were no Stone Age wars. We just call them migrations. They were conflicts between territorial groups fighting for 2-D SPACE. That kind of behavior goes way back to Mammalia. When people-sized tribes compete, the advantage goes to the people that work together more cohesively. The best memes for a people foster cooperation. Tribes have a *loyalty* characteristic that measures the willingness of their members to contribute to tribal success. Good memes enhance cooperation and raise the tribe's loyalty score.

Language borders

In the Stone Age, their language put the most natural boundary around a People. These days, a common language is not required, as in Canada or Switzerland. Shared memes outweigh a shared language for those countries. More commonly, as with Spanish or Arabic, the speakers share a common language but are different enough to be separate peoples. Distinct peoples might speak the same language if both peoples were subjects of the same empire. The language outlasted the empire. Previous empirical borders may not line up with the peoples now separated or enclosed by them. Such borders force incompatible peoples to cohabitate within illogical borders. Conflict is likely if the bonds within each tribe are strong.

Modern peoples

The distinction between the peoples of the world was clearer when language was the only consideration. "*We* speak a language *They* don't." We assume here that the number of Stone Age Peoples is equal to the number of languages in the world before the agriculture meme emerged. There have been many mergers and extinctions since then, leaving about 7000 languages currently. A great deal of merging and sharing has taken place in the last 5000 years. Empires have spread their core languages outwardly, overrunning local languages in many cases. In others, the language remains extant. People that can keep their language are the best bet for forming an independent country of their own when the empire falls. For some peoples, that situation won't be the first time that the empires above them have come and gone. Many peoples have experienced empire, sometimes from the top, which they remember fondly. Those consistently on the bottom have other memories.

Minority peoples

A People can still be a significant minority tribe without their original language. Minorities can be the remnant of conquered peoples, including slaves. They no longer have a homeland that they control. A homeland is the first "possession" of a people. They might still have their own language, in which case, their probability of regaining control of their homeland is greatly enhanced. If they lose their homeland and their language, all they have left are minor memes and lore. Such a people are but a remnant of their former selves. Success in keeping the remnants of the old tribe together reflects on the stickiness of their memes. Individuals that *assimilate* give up their major memes in favor of the dominant culture's memes.

Ethnic minorities

An *ethnic* minority has genetic characteristics distinct enough that the members of the dominant culture can label them *Other* by sight. Members of the dominant tribe can exclude others from full participation in the tribe, demoting them to second class citizenship. Assimilation is harder, but genetic mixing will occur. The boundaries blur, but it takes a while. Changing the memes would be quicker. Memes are electric and rapidly adjustable. Genes are chemical and slow.

Strength of Tribe

There are degrees of "Peopleness". The most successful peoples have a country with firm borders that they defend, and a justice system judged acceptably fair by its citizens. In short, they control, as much as possible, their own destiny. The weakest peoples have no memes that anyone follows anymore. In between are minority *communities* with a variable strength of bond. Some have survived empire better than others. Some are still inside an empire but might recover control over their own fate someday.

Remnant peoples

There are many societies that are mere remnants of their former selves. They just weren't strong enough to keep it together. Such tribes are leaky. Their members opt out and adopt the behaviors (memes) of the winners. If the genetics aren't too obvious, they learn to blend into the dominant culture rather quickly. If they "anglicize" their names, one of the last pieces of the old culture is gone.

New World Tribes

People-shaped Tribes often emerge when nascent peoples get tired of empires. European empires (Spain, England, and Portugal) conquered the New World and Australia, then lost control to the colonists. New *Peoples* like Americans and Mexicans emerged. They inherited most of their memes from Britain and Iberia, of course.

Tribal fate

There are many Stone Age tribes that are completely gone. Note that genetic heritage is seldom lost[101] because some stragglers survive. Many gene

[101] Tasmanians excepted. Islands can trap gene sets. Cuba may be the largest island "cleansed" of native genes.

lines in an empire come from extinct peoples whose last members joined the empire. Between barbarian rape and imperial slavery, few Stone Age genes are completely gone. But the language, the rites, and the lore that made them a culturally unique people are gone. We can track genes well enough to locate regions of ethnicity, though we may not know the languages or even names of those lost tribes. We can usually track the Main Sequence of successful peoples back to the Stone Age. They responded to barbarians and empire by forming a kingdom. They may or may not have been under the thumb of empire more than once. They may have *been* the empire. The smart/adaptable/flexible societies then hopped aboard the Trust meme to join in the Age of Plenty. Where to go from there? Society is a complex adaptive system. Prediction is iffy, at best.

The Newest People

The remnant tribes described above started with a homeland, a language, and a cultural memory. There is one minority people that started with *none* of these. Africans arrived in the Americas as tribeless individuals and had to construct their tribe from scratch. They lost their languages and even their names. Very little African culture survived the crossing. How many Haley families have a Kunta

Kinte remnant memory? Family names may be the last remnants of many lost cultures.

A People born after the Stone Age

Starting from scratch is a unique way to build a People and definitely off the Main Sequence. The history of Africans in America demonstrates many of the principles of complexity science: self-organization, emergence, and evolution. It is rare for a people to emerge with virtually no memes at all. That is the case with African Americans. First, all the individual slaves shipped from Africa lost *all* their Tribes. They lost their Family, Band, and People. They lost their language and religion and memes for how they are expected to interact with other people. They even lost their family *name* and took the name of their master along with his language. All the culture that remained of their former tribes, all that survived the crossing, was scraps of lore. Of course, they preserved their genetic information, which was distinctive enough to form a We/They boundary between black and white. This is a case where membership in a tribe is less than fully voluntary, which is possible with any distinctive ethnic difference. You may not consider yourself part of a tribe, but other tribes might. In that sense, white Americans mostly thought of black Americans as

They. The free blacks were not fully accepted but were perhaps better off before the civil War than after. Jim Crow laws cemented their second-class citizenship. That might have been a downgrade for free blacks but was an upgrade for former slaves.

Can't share memes when you're locked up

The isolated slaves on a plantation, being social critters, would form a very local community (We) but nothing larger than a Band. Slaves could barely communicate with other plantations, so the opportunity to build a People couldn't even begin until they were freed. The free blacks had a head start but before the Civil War had barely started bonding into a distinct people. Colleges for free blacks emerged just before the war as the first major *institutions* to emerge in support of Afro-American individuals. They taught western memes, not African American culture, which hardly existed yet.

100 years in second class

After 1865, the freed slaves began to self-organize, as all social critters do. They needed memes and institutions. They got those from American culture. Cultural appropriation is a convenient way to get a head start on building a tribe. Why reinvent the wheel? Copy the behavior of a successful tribe! The former slaves were already Christian, so churches, as recognizably distinct institutions, emerged first. The free blacks had a head start on that other American/Western meme–free enterprise. The newly freed slaves often opted for sharecropping, a not very lucrative form of free enterprise. There weren't a lot of other opportunities. Music allowed one avenue for distinctive cultural expression. Gospel may have been the first recognizable African American thing. More musical forms emerged later. Jazz came out of New Orleans, as did Creole and Cajun cooking, which is about half French and half Black. Music remains a major component of a distinct African American culture. Much of the rest comes from Western culture, specifically American and Christian memes, with a recent dash of Islam.

Full citizenship

As a case study of a society starting from nothing, the African American experience is unique. They started with no memes, so had to either develop their own or borrow some. The first survival behavior they adopted was the subservience of a slave. They didn't lose all those behaviors when freed, when they graduated from slavery to second class citizens. They still looked down when spoken to, for instance. Over the next century, they learned western ways. It took a century for the majority culture in America (mislabeled "white") to accept them as full citizens. The law changed because a major American Xeno meme changed. America accepted Them as part of We in a legal and binding sense after the Civil Rights Act.

Race is not a Tribe

Advocates for African American progress might claim that they support progress for their *race*, but there is no memory mechanism for each race. Also, those advocates do not speak for residents of Africa or the Caribbean. Race is not a tribe but a genetic characteristic. Membership in a tribe, not defined by ethnicity, is voluntary in that you can always quit that tribe. There is no genetic contract that an individual can opt out of. There is an *African American* culture (and social contract) based on *ethnicity*. Ethnicity is a combination of cultural (behavioral) and genetic distinctiveness, either of which can trigger a We/They reaction. They are also separable. Having Caucasian genes does not commit a person to "white" memes. There are no memes that unite all members of a race. The memes attributed to "whiteness" are the memes of Western civilization. Russians are Caucasian but not western. They never absorbed the trust meme, the main Western meme.

Japan and other Asian peoples did. This doesn't mean Russians are barbarians, but they have, quite recently, invaded their neighbors to expand their empire. That's a pretty good clue.

Race vs ethnicity

Scholars have often argued that race is an artificial distinction. "There is only one race, the human race." Humans are a subclass of Species. The only qualification for membership in a species is sexual interoperability. Mating pairs of critters that produce viable young are of the same species. (Some flexible DNA lines like *genus* Canis Lupis–wolves and dogs–are interfertile. Humans aren't that close to the other apes.) There are hundreds of dog breeds but only three races? Dogs are recognizably different breeds. Are there hundreds of visibly different ethnicities? Can a Kazakh spot the differences from afar between a Portuguese and a Greek? Recognizable differences can trigger an instinctive We/They reaction. There are memes, cultured behaviors, which temper our Stranger/Danger reaction. It's called being civilized. Some ethnicities have caught the Ag and City memes only recently. The closer they are to the Stone Age, the worse they do on standardized tests. This can be a totally cultural issue or part genetic, if survival of the fittest kicks in.

Cities are stressful, but are they dangerous enough that a stupid hunter can't survive in the city or on the farm? Every ethnicity has a story. Races don't. There's no tribe for sex, either. Feminists are members of an *Advocacy* tribe. Nobody speaks for all women on Earth.

Army, the First Institution

Barbarians emerge.

The Barbarian meme provided the original impetus for the *Army*. A mob of hungry guys *emerged* as a tribe when they learned a certain trick for survival (involving robbery and associated mayhem) AND taught those lessons to the next generation. Note that the next generation doesn't necessarily mean those soldiers' sons. In the Army, it's the next batch of recruits. A tribe must Replenish() lost members to achieve tribal immortality. This can happen faster in an army than any other tribe. Not many tribes have graves registration specialists. Not all tribes have named leaders. Bands need one but *Peoples* don't, except in times of trouble. The Army has one, with the title of General.

```
class Army extends Tribe {
  Set Purpose='Kill people and take things'
//Attribute    Data Type    Comment
  General      Member       // Upgraded Alpha
//Methods
  KillPeople( ) {...}
  TakeThings( ) {...}
  BreakThings( ) {...}   }  // The modern meme
```

From fireside chat to SOP

The main claim to cultural tribalhood is that tribes conserve information and pass it on to the next generation. In modern times, an Army has SOPs, field manuals, and "lessons learned." Back in the past, they had soldiers telling stories around the campfire. Close enough.

A top-down structure

The Army formalized the hierarchical tree as its control structure. In Stone Age Bands, talent would generally bubble to the top, but the structure was less rigid. A general invented the top-down model. The king, emperor, and company president borrowed it. It is an effective behavior for control of a tribe that is in pursuit of a clear goal.

The Army serves the people (or not).

The Army, at best, serves as the strong *right* arm of the city-state, empire, kingdom or nation in defending against threats from afar. The strong *left* (long) arm of the land-holding tribes covers miscreants inside the borders. Everyone but the generals and the King/Dictator consider using the army for the purpose of justice a bad meme.

The modern army purpose

The modern army has the goal of killing people and breaking things. The pure Barbarian meme is to kill people and *take* things. Armies still specialize in causing loss. Humans more commonly organize and work together to prevent loss or, in a positive-sum game, to create value and make things better. The army exists to destroy lives and break *their* valuables or, in the defense, to destroy lives and prevent breakage of *our* valuables. The Army has seen changes in its basic mission. The first purpose was to take food from the neighbors. If a few of them died, too bad. Threatening them was cheaper since killing the farmers reduces next year's crop. Killing soldiers, of course, still makes sense. Imperial memes had the Army taking land and slaves instead of just crops. Of course, they took anything else that wasn't nailed down. In modern armies, that behavior has nearly died, which was very nice of them. Now, in the Age of Plenty, instead of *taking* things, the Army *breaks* things. Our inter-networked wealth generation system is easier to break. Armies have always been interested in breaking walls. Now they break bridges and roads. The Roman army built roads rather than wrecked them, but the Romans were weird.

A new mission

The newest emergent behavior is to assign humanitarian missions to the army. Noone ever designed an army for that purpose. It is quite out of character. Armies have assets (trucks) that can help in disasters, but any time spent training for such missions takes away from the core mission. If it causes the army not to Survive(), that's a bad thing for that local instance of Army. It won't kill the *class* Army. The class of tribe named Army does not seem in danger of obsolescence or extinction. Specific instances of the class, however, can Expire().

City-State, the First Type of Country

The Hamlet, a failed meme

The Hamlet meme worked for the first farmers until barbarian armies made that tribal form untenable. The transition between the Stone Age and Age of Empire happened from 10,000 to 5,000 years ago. That was Conan's time, the Hyperborean Age. The Hamlet suffered a mismatch in scale with the new environment. Farmers needed an upgrade to survive. They needed a people-sized response, and the people formed a *Country*.

City walls work

The first upgrade was the *City*. It emerged to defend against barbarian armies. The city-state was the first *Country*, a uber-category of tribe that includes empires, kingdoms, and modern nations. It is usually the only tribe that can take your life for violating the social contract. All tribes need a justice system. The punishment varies. Stone Age bands would usually just exile a miscreant, which was pretty close to a death sentence. A Stone Age People seldom organized themselves well enough to put someone to death for violating the social contract. The Band might.

```
class Country extends Tribe          {
 {set Purpose='Administer the Homeland'
  set ToDieFor=True[102]}
//Attribute    Data Type    Comment
  Homeland     Area         // Upgraded territory
  Defenders    Army         // The good Army
  Leader       Elder        // Fearless
  Citizens[103] List[Human]// not just Warm
//Methods
Adjudicate(Death) {...}     // Max tribal fee
Defend(Homeland) {...}
RaiseTaxes( ) {...}   }     // To pay the Defenders
```

Defend the Homeland

Kingdoms, nations, and empires share a core requirement to defend the homeland. The city transferred the defensive function to the *Country* long ago.[104] The city-state was something of a fad. The city survives for a different purpose now. They remain of value because they maximize human interaction. This is where social evolution proceeds at the fastest rate, a considerable advantage in the competition to

[102] *"It is sweet and proper to die for one's country." Horace*

[103] Not necessarily "civilized" citizens of a *City*

[104] Except for Monaco and a few others, up to Uruguay

survive and prosper. They operate closer to the Edge of Chaos, where evolution proceeds most rapidly.

```
class City extends Country{ // My kind of town
 {set Purpose = "Defend the walls"
   if after(getDate('Greek Unification'))
     {set ToDieFor = False
       set Purpose="Promote interactions"}}
```

Cities, the second complex adaptive system

Cities are also a prime example of a complex adaptive system, and is, in fact, the second system, after species, recognized by the young discipline of complexity science. Cities provide a prime example of unplanned growth, a key characteristic of complex adaptive systems. Attempts to impose urban planning on cities have not often gone well. Complexity science suggests that trying to *direct* the evolution of any "living" system is fraught with peril.

Long live the city

Cities are also among the most long-lasting tribes. Many kingdoms and empires have died around the same cities. Allegiance to this kind of tribe has waned. At first, the citizens manned the city walls, which leads to a deeper level of bonding than in cities of today. The defense function shifted outward to king, then (maybe) nation, but the City was the first Country and had the first Taxman. Loyalty shifted from the city to the "outer" tribe when the defense responsibility moved. You can still be loyal to a city's baseball team, though. The requirements of membership in the fan club are far less than they once were. Membership in a city once required you to man the walls when the enemy came to town. Now you don't even have to show up at the game. The city has been demoted from a country with ToDieFor=True to a (weak) community, loyalty-wise. Institutionally, the city remains a distinct jurisdiction within a country, with its own local cops. In that respect, the American states (a tribal class not defined here) have lost a bit of loyalty since the Civil War days.

Country, the Tribe with a Stick

Government tribes at all levels have two methods of getting their members to behave: the Carrot and the Stick. We allow few classes of Tribe to use lethal sticks. (The Mafia is not "allowed" but its members accept violence, up to and including death, as a legitimate form of conflict resolution.) The government has a stick by consent of the governed. The *Country* has evolved to apply the stick effectively over the last 5000 years. It has less experience with carrots.

Kingdom, a People's Response to Barbarians

Stone Age war

In the Stone Age, a *People* was a loose collection of bands. They might appoint a war chief to lead in times of trouble. A Stone Age people on offense or defense would be more of a *Swarm* than an *Army*. A swarm has no effective memory, so is not a tribe. It doesn't even last long enough to be a Mob. (Herds can last millennia. Migratory flocks last only a few weeks, so they are a swarm. A dolphin super-pod is a similar temporary mob.) Historians often call long-term competition between Stone Age peoples a "migration" rather than a war. Low-level, long-term competition might not even need a war chief. The band chieftains of a more aggressive people might act on their own. A migration driven by environmental change, most often a reduction in available food for one reason or another (abbreviated "drought"), can force a more collective response among the chieftains. But War Chief is a temporary position. There is no permanent sub-tribe of full-time warriors to save any lessons learned. However, each band can retain a few tricks and the People.Remember() the best stories. They are amateurs. The serious retention of martial lessons began with the *Army*.

A new threat

Barbarian armies represent a permanent environmental threat. The occasional war chief morphs to permanent king. A *Kingdom* has more cohesion than a *People* because the threat is more-or-less permanent. Among the ties that bind, fighting shoulder to shoulder for your life ranks high. The people-sized tribe called Kingdom became something to die for. (That was the default for the Country class, so doesn't need to be redefined here.)

Kings emerge in response to Empires

```
class Kingdom extends Country{
 {set Purpose='God save the King'}
//Attribute     Data Type     Comment
 King           Family        // Not just a Member
 Nobles         List[Family]  // Upper class
 Commoners      List[Members]
// Methods
 Bequeath(Crown) {...} }      // Royal parameter
```

Powers of the King

A King has more power than any "Leader of the People" of the Stone Age. In peacetime, an effective leader of a Stone Age people would not even exist. The chiefs might select a War Chief for defense of the homeland, but he would not retain kinglike powers after the war. (An aggressive stone age leader, say Chaka Zulu, is more of an emperor wannabe than a king.) The King can call the people to war on offense or defense. In addition to handling external threats, the king has vastly more control over *internal* threats, that is, injustices within the tribe. The King disseminates justice high and low. He delegates local constabulary responsibilities to his nobles. He has power over the local nobles (but not the "super-tribe" Aristocracy, defined later. That is international in scope. They don't have a leader and don't answer to anyone.)

A Family affair

The habit of bequeathing power along family lines did not begin with kings. The chief of a Native American band might expect his son to become the next chief. Kings were just more formal about it. Note that the one member of the tribe with the title King is an individual, but his Family owns the throne.

Borders, a subset of written Law

A king controls a *Country*. A stone age People control a *Territory*. A country's border is better defined and more stable than a people's territory. Officially negotiated borders existed in the Age of Empire, but the Treaties of Westphalia made borders even more firm. Those were the political start of the Age of Plenty. They established a sovereignty meme in law rather than custom. Much of the progress of the West comes from transitioning from custom to written law, more in terms of internal justice than border integrity. Writing emerged in the Age of Empire and is essential for controlling the empire. Kings can be illiterate in comparison.

Modern Kingdoms

Kingdoms still exist for peoples that have opted *against* the Trust meme. The modern version of King is Dictator. He still wants his son to inherit his power, so the Family "owns" the throne. One big difference is that the new aristocracy supporting the "Leader of the People" is not entirely based on blood. You can become a Colonel (the new Duke) through competent ruthlessness. Modern Kingdoms are meritocracies!

Empire

AKA "Evil Empire"

```
class Empire extends Country      { // Evil (adj)
  {set Purpose='Expand the Homeland'}
//Attribute     Data Type      Comment
  Emperor       Family         // King-like
  Nobles        List[Family]   //Upper class
//Methods
  Conquer( ) {...}             // Prosper in 2-D SPACE
  Dominate( ) {...}   }        // Lord it over Them
```

Empire.Prosper(SPACE)

An *Empire* usually centers on a city. The Mongols were a notable exception. Empires demonstrate a core characteristic of groups of critters. Groups try to expand in 2D SPACE. Every species tries to extend its range. A pack will try to extend its hunting territory. A ministry wants to increase its flock. All LivingThings want to grow. Critters need to grow enough to spawn the next generation. Empires want land. Then they stay and rule as long as they can by dominating the local peoples.

The limits to growth

As discussed previously, groups don't "want" things the same way individuals do. The "desire" to grow is simply an unchecked positive feedback loop, not an emotion. The environment provides limits to growth. This includes other groups competing for the same things. Without the desire to grow, the group will not survive the competitive nature of life on Earth. There are no half-measures. No group grows then stops of its own volition. They will only stop if opposed.

National growth

Modern nations are more peaceful than empires in this respect, but not immune to the urge to grow. They generally don't invade other nations, kingdoms, or empires unless provoked. They respect formal borders. Kings and emperors have borders. Stone Age peoples don't. If they don't have borders, maybe you're not invading. Native American and Australian tribes didn't have kings, so their lands were fair game. Empires invade and dominate the inhabitants. Nations invade and kick the inhabitants out. Ethnic cleansing provides more stability.

The American empire

The Americans tried empire after the Spanish-American war. We weren't very good at it. We easily gave up the Philippines and the Panama Canal.[105] The other Western (ship-based) empires had hundreds of years of experience and gave up their empires with considerably more fuss. Land-based, contiguous empires still haven't given up. The non-western Russians and Chinese are slow to trust and slower to transition out of empire mode.

Empires are still making trouble.

Most recent conflicts have been between empires. WWII pitted the British and Russian empires against the Japanese and wannabe German empires. The French, Italians, Chinese, and Dutch had empires, but they were minor players. At the time, the US held the Philippines but calling them an empire is a stretch. All the parties involved, except the Chinese and Russians, had adopted the Trust meme and were on the path to nationhood. The next scale of conflict–a sort of hybrid–was between an *Empire* and a *Civilization*. The Cold War pitted the Soviets against the West. If the Chinese had wholeheartedly

[105] That was stupid!

joined, it would have been a conflict between Civilizations. They didn't, so it was just the Soviets spouting Marxist memes at the West. As a form of LivingThing, the Soviets, of course, wanted to grow. It could use the standard Empire.Conquer() method until the end of WWII. Then they tried a remote empire, using memes (and bribery) instead of gunboats. Cuba was their best shot, but the Soviets didn't last. That tribe has started calling itself Russia, again. It also started expanding once more. It's an old habit.

Aristocracy

The emergence of an upper class

The Aristocracy is a Tribe composed of upper-class members of several empires or kingdoms. Stone Age societies were/are basically classless. The nobility separates some members of the tribe from others with distinctive behaviors and privileges. The Aristocracy is a super-Tribe that (semi) unites the nobility from each kingdom and empire. They are united in privileged behavior and by marriage. The *Aristocracy* is a child of *Tribe*, not *Country*. It is super-national, for one thing. The individual members (families) have day jobs. They owe allegiance to their local King or Emperor. They have superpowers at home. The international super-tribe, the "Upper Class" as a whole, has little enforcement authority. It doesn't even have a leader. It's more of a *community*.

```
class Aristocracy extends Tribe{ // International
   {set Purpose='Preserve our privilege'}
//Attribute    Data Type      Comment
 Nobility      List[Family] // Connected
//Methods
 Marry(Well) {...}   }       // Tribal boundary
```

Great users of blades

The original nobles were the best barbarians. The king or emperor rewarded them with land and privilege for their martial prowess. They developed a multi-level hierarchical tree modeled after the army's officer corps, but with a king at the top rather than a general. The captains of war took on duties as tax collectors and judges and punishers. They wielded the Stick of Justice, with a license to kill, in the Age of Empire. They defined the boundary of the nobility and separated themselves from the peasants with their marriage customs. They had access to exotic goods from afar as one of their privileges. The opportunities for conspicuous consumption and pageantry improved in the Age of Plenty, as *Nations* emerged and the power of the nobility declined. The primary goal of the aristocratic tribe, as a community of similarly inclined individuals, was to maintain their position of superiority over the peasants.

Commonality with Others

The aristocratic tribe reached across borders. A French baron had more in common with a Russian duke than with a French peasant. They'd marry a foreigner, for instance. Such exclusiveness sets an obvious boundary to the Tribe. There are other behaviors that distinguish members of the aristocracy. They assumed an inherent superiority over the peasantry, based on blood (because they didn't know what genes were). They had a rather unique meme called chivalry, which may be more PR than fact. They had princesses...their best PR gambit.

A new aristocracy?

We often label the members of the Age of Plenty's nouveau riche the new aristocracy, but there are differences. Such new "aristocrats" were also called robber barons, but they aren't that, either. The original robber barons were medieval toll takers on the Rhine. They added no value to trade along the river. They were barbarians. It was the Age of Empire, after all. The "barons" of industry *created* value – in huge amounts. They advanced the Age of Plenty more than any other sector of humanity. The elite of the Industrial Age (roughly the latter half of the Age of Plenty) became super rich by taking effective advantage of the new forms of ENERGY that became available. They also needed to be better at math and logic than the standard barbarian, who could reach the nobility on charisma and emotion. The math requirement is part of the continuously increasing importance of INFORMATION in our lives. Every SOP that increases humanity's ability to Reshape(Matter) adds to the encyclopedia of knowledge that enhances our lives. Industrialists planned and organized and reshaped best. They are part of the 2.5% Elite on the high end of the Klutz axis.

Differences, now and then

The Industrial Age upper class is not the same tribe as the old nobility. They don't control the serfs, and they don't have police powers. The new barons are elite in capability, as were the original imperial barons. They had different purposes, but both were very good at organizing people and getting things done. The task changed from fighting to trading, but both activities allow the best talent to rise to the top. However, elite fathers do not necessarily sire elite children. Mediocre kids can maintain the realm for a while. However, the pace of activity is greater in the Age of Plenty, so turnover is higher. Mobility up and down the class structure is higher now. The new version of aristocracy has less exclusive memes for cross-class marriage. A pretty starlet has better prospects for a ring than a pretty peasant.

Tribal qualifications

The new upper-class tribe might differ from the old but still might be a tribe, if it meets the qualifications. Does it have a memory, a distinctive culture, and a social contract? Is it immortal? Do its memes help the tribe survive and prosper? Is this new tribe different enough from the old aristocracy that we need a new name for it? Are these the new Elites? Are they the Privileged? Recall that Elite was defined previously as the most competent people you've ever met. The use of the word Elite for members born into the upper class is aggravating when it is unearned. Being born into the InCrowd isn't good enough. We reserve the term Elite for the top 2.5 % of *capable* people two standard deviations or more above the norm. (Six standard deviations out and you're a superstar.[106]) You have earned any privileges you get. Birthright doesn't make you elite, just

[106] "Redford and Streisand. That's it!" Mike Meyers, @SNL

privileged. The Elite earn their privileges (or should in a fair society). They're the ones who get 'er done.

The InCrowd

The InCrowd in the Age of Plenty is a combination of old money and new talent. The newbies aren't necessarily as snooty as the old aristocrats. Old money is more likely to follow that old meme. The members of any upper class tend to worry more about status than the peons, for whom Survive() is closer to home than Prosper(). The InCrowd is still highly invested in maintaining its privileges. They no longer have the arm of the law, so they can just chide and exclude. We'll see how far that gets them. They tend to use information as their weapon of choice, rather than the solid MATTER of barbarian blades. INFORMATION is getting more and more important in our lives, so we may yet see a new round of *Aristocracy,* one with a different Stick.

Nations

Nations are an Age of Plenty version of the People. Many of the "nations" in the United Nations are dictatorships, which are structurally indistinguishable from Kingdoms. Since the dictator remains in power, this form of government still reflects the will and the memes of the people.

The Age of Nations (@alt.age)

```
class Nation extends Country        {// "Western"
  {set Purpose=' Live Free or Die!'}
//Methods
Vote( ) {...}
DoGood( ) {...} }       // Progressive projects
```

Kings create nations (not that they meant to).

The modern nation-state emerged (became sovereign in a very legal and binding sense)[107] with the Treaties of Westphalia (c. 1648). The kings who signed the treaties certainly did not expect that this act would help doom them and the aristocracy. Such is the nature of new (emergent) behaviors in complex adaptive systems. The new behaviors are unplanned and often surprising.

[107] Ref. Swamp baron @HolyGrail

Other ducks in the row

1648 is the political start of the Age of Plenty, but there are other factors. The legal impetus began with Roman jurisprudence. Written law is older than Rome, but the Romans normalized *precedent*, which added stability, consistency, and fairness to the justice system. Western nations adopted Roman legal memes and the Greek memes for democracy. Many people think those were good ideas. Aristocratic wannabes want a return to a two-tiered society, with them in charge, of course. (But are they ruthless enough?)

Middle class values

The middle-class votes for *Nation* over kingdom or empire. The middle-class supports the nation more enthusiastically than peasants ever did the king or emperor. The middle-class invented patriotism, a step higher than fealty to the King in the level of members' commitment to the tribe. Nations are worth fighting for because the middle class has skin in the game.

Government power tools

Government tribes at all levels have two methods of getting their members to behave: the Carrot and the Stick. Aside from the Army and Country, we grant few tribes lethal sticks. *Institutions* can punish bad behavior with fines or suspensions. *Communities* can only snarl at you. The government has a lethal stick by consent of the governed, as a unique part of its social contract. The *Country* has evolved to apply the stick effectively over the last 5000 years. It has less experience with Carrots. We can consider the Royal Mail, as an aid to commerce, to be a carrot. The Royal Mint is older and still carries a lot of status in determining which societies are the Big Boys[108]. This is more civilized than the Empire meme where your Country.Status rating relied on your ability to beat the hell out of your neighbors. A more effective carrot may be the King's Road meme, wherein building roads is a collective effort for the common good, even if the king is dead. Long live his road.

The King's road

Defending the border is the first responsibility of the King. In pursuit of that, he could keep up

[108] Reaching space is the newest status symbol.

the roads and charge it to the defense budget even before there were budgets. State sponsored road/bridge improvements for the purpose of enhanced *commerce* is an Age of Plenty meme. The Romans paved the way but for soldiers more than merchants. The clan system does not support the King's Road meme. The modern nation has inherited the King's Road meme and spread it to its subdivisions. Western citizens are taxed to "level the way" by their city, county, state, and nation (the "layers" of countryhood). Canal and railroad companies reduced other travel impediments at no cost to the taxpayer. Airplanes apparently can't do that. Air traffic control is now a standard country-sized Carrot. Rail travel has also migrated to the federal government almost everywhere. The port authorities are still local, so expect the "responsible" Bureau (tribe) to Grow() in their direction next.

Do-gooders

The Nation is distinct from previous forms of governance in that it consistently tries to do good. Emperors and kings are not known for this trait. Their schedule was full of defense and justice issues. A few built roads and bridges that enhanced, sometimes only incidentally, the welfare of the tribe. A few built universities or mints. Nations picked up on those and added more, starting with public education. The public education meme came from the grass roots. Some Christian sects wanted people to read the Bible. (The Church should get more credit than the King for public education.) This focus on education (from the Hebrew) was so effective in a tribe's Prosper() efforts that empires were forced to adopt it. Otherwise, they could not keep up with nations. Emperors and the new kings (dictators) use top-down education to control their populations, which betrays their barbaric roots. The top-down approach has become more prevalent as the Age of Plenty has aged. In the U.S. we started with local (grass roots) schoolmarms, then invented state universities. Now the feds pull the strings. Given the current state of American education, we may have centralized a bit too much. The Department of Education's declared intent is "fairness", but it results in conformity. Maximal societal progress would, instead, come from fifty separate departments. A centralized approach is not "robust" as the complexity scientists say. Grandma says you're putting all your eggs in one centralized basket. During Covid, more baskets emerged, but the Swedes jumped out. Good for them. Sovereignty is superior to conformity.

The Government is here to help.

Nations have found more ways to DoGood(). The US borrowed from the successful King's Road and Royal Mail memes. They added a Bureau of Standards just for the Measurement meme.[109] In the US Constitution, these come under "promote the general welfare." The king didn't have that clause in his contract. After defense and justice, the "normal" functions of a nation now include mail, roads, and coin. The federal level in the US did not address education until 1979. Most new federal departments added between 1789 and 1953 have been justice related, including Interior, Commerce, and Labor. (We founded the Department of Agriculture to DoGood() as a Lab+Library tribe in 1862.) Only after 1953, with the creation of the Department of Health, Education, and Welfare, did the new departments concentrate on new forms of do-gooding. We can ascribe some of their activities to risk prevention–preventing people from doing dangerous things. Risk prevention has huge potential for finding things to fix, enabling the Bureau.Grow() method. Another form of risk prevention involves the Federal Reserve. Its purpose is to DoGood() by dampening the swings of the "natural" Boom/Bust

[109] The Navy kept the Clock.

cycle. However, the Market is a complex system, so successful control is dubious. If it works, it provides "stability", which is actually counter-productive if the goal is to make the country stronger as fast as possible. It's a move away from chaos and toward Island Life, away from the sweet spot of evolution that keeps your tribe competitive. In addition, it doesn't always work. The dike springs too many leaks for your fingers. The Law of Unintended Consequences looms large in any attempt to control a complex system. But control freaks still believe in the Clockwork Universe. It will be hard to convince them to give up the reins. They'll never give up the *concept* of reins.

Super Tribes

Multi-People organizations over the years

There is one *voluntary* form of togetherness that is larger than a People or Country, the *Civilization*. Empires can be just as large, but the subjected peoples did not volunteer to join. The two current ones on Earth are Islam and Western civilization. Egypt had an empire, not a civilization. China has always been an empire. Christian peoples, a tribe formed to oppose the Islamic Empire, have mostly adopted Western memes. The medieval Christian super-tribe has dissolved. Of the other major religions, Buddhism comes closest in uniting separate peoples into a super tribe, which is not very much. Marxism was no more successful. The Chinese and Russian Marxist empires mouthed the dogma but never really got along.

A (weak) community of Tribes

Super-tribes are groups of tribes that follow the same memes. A civilization has no specific point of memory retention. It might have a Book. The Bible, Koran, and Communist Manifesto serve as a rallying point for international communities. Super-tribes have few legal means of enforcement. Its members behave because they follow the memes of their civilization. Super-tribes get a minimal amount of loyalty from the members, who have minimal duties. They do a minimal amount of inter-people justice and don't have much authority to punish disobedience. In this, they are like a *community*, the weakest level of tribes, despite their size. They can chide and exclude. They have a social contract, but don't provide a lot of service, so getting voted off the island doesn't hurt much, unless you are in a super-guild of guilds. A doctor defying the WHO might be in trouble.

Alliances are usually Swarms

Alliances between land defense entities are usually temporary groups of class Swarm. Individual tribes (countries) can retain the lessons learned, but there is no permanent shared library. An alliance is more of an *event* than an organization. NATO is old enough to be a separate tribe. It has a specific knowledge repository, potentially a "Lessons Learned" office. Mere continuity is enough to spark an unspecific retention process, as in Tales around the Campfire.[110] NATO also has more teeth than book-driven super-tribes, strong enough to be label it an *Institution*. It can levy fines on non-compliant members, for instance. NATO is a super-tribe with standard tribal desires. It wants to Survive() and Prosper(). Prosper most commonly means grow, as NATO did, especially after the Soviet empire collapsed. It might seem odd that NATO expanded as the threat diminished. Unconstrained tribes will do that.

Artificial Tribes

The United Nations is an artificial attempt to form a tribe. "Natural" tribes emerged without conscious

[110] Old school

planning. The natural forms of land-holding tribe that have emerged since the Stone Age are *Clan*, *Kingdom*, *Empire*, and *Nation*. Stone Age *Peoples* that survived but haven't formed one of those are now an ethnic minority within one of those. The United "Nations" is a collection empires, kingdoms, nations, and failed states ("organized" in clans). The European Union is another conscious attempt to create a super-tribe by law. The EU can do more than chastise to punish misbehavior. That would put them in the class of institutional tribes. They aren't in the ToDieFor power class (yet), but they want to be. They would love to overtop the power of the sovereign nations. They want to grow. That's what Groups of critters do. Should the EU come to dominate, European nations will no longer be sovereign. The situation would resemble an empire with a dominating class less ethnically distinct than usual. The best candidate for a ruling class is the *InCrowd*, a less xenophobic version of the *Aristocracy*.

Clans

At the edge of Empire

The last (or maybe the first) of the major organizational forms man has tried since the Bronze Age is the Clan. It comes from the Herder meme rather than the Agriculture meme. Most of the Ag meme tribes went with Kings. Animal herders were more footloose and less amenable to central authority. Farmers can follow most the animal husbandry memes, including some unavailable to nomads like Coop(). Nomads inhabited less fertile lands, so attracted less imperial attention. They are off the main roads and don't get as much practice at dealing with outsiders. They don't have "civilized" memes for cooperating with Them because they don't get to the city that often. Nomads absorbed some Barbarian memes.[111] The most successful nomadic empires were the Mongol and Islamic. Islam had more staying power, partly by moving into cities. Thus, they kept up with the Joneses (Christians) until the Trust meme propelled the West out of feudalism. Islam's best Civilization.Grow() meme was converting its conquered non-believers via taxation. Clans are still prevalent in the Islamic world and still in competition with its kings/dictators. Clans command considerably less loyalty within modern nations, to the point of being merely ceremonial.

[111] but who didn't? The only Tribes that avoided them are the Uncontacted.

"What we have here is a failure to organize."

In Failed States, warlords don't have a country. They have a territory. They share this with other warlords in an ungovernable region that might be the result of British/French statesmanship. Their diplomatic goal was to establish (remote) control by enclosing three peoples within one border and supporting a weak king to "rule" over them. Some of the "nations" in the United Nations still reflect that late-stage imperial strategy. They are not *Nations* as defined here. Nations adopted the Trust meme. Clans didn't. Failed States are still a people or three, most of whom are very late to the Ag and City memes. Their interactions with other peoples have mainly been with empires. They are not fond of central authority in any form. They prefer the clan system, as evidenced by their consistent rejection of any other form. On the Control Stack, clans are anarchists.

King and Clan

Clans rejected kings and emperors in many places but gave way in others. English history records a struggle with King defeating Clan as the primary organizational form. It also demonstrates a Tribe evolving and accepting a more centralized form for the sake of their People.Survive() method. Clans that accepted a King move up a notch on the Control Stack. They lose political power but still have their lore. Their clan was demoted from the ToDieFor level of commitment to a *community* with some lore[112] to talk about. Clans that won (over king or empire) remain convinced their path is correct. They drift down on the Control Stack with each success. The Afghan clans are the best current example of tribes on the bottom end of stack. They've been at it since Alexander.

Non-territorial Tribes

Except for the Civilization the tribal forms discussed above relate to homeland defense, even Family if all else fails. (The Army is not technically territorial. The King is. We introduced the Army above in chronological order of emergence, as the first "artificial" tribe.) Humans are territorial and we need to organize to defend our territory. The various types of tribes mentioned above describe how we have organized for that critical function. Other kinds of tribes have different goals. Those that survived have evolved to fulfill those functions better and better over time. They include formal *institutions*

[112] Including Scottish tartans

and looser *communities*. Individual institutions like museums or universities are local tribes, with possible super-tribes uniting them. How strongly local tribes conform to any super-tribe memes above them differs. Religious tribes can be bound tightly. Museums or libraries seem quite independent of any national or international coordinating agencies. Professors and reporters have recently become more subservient to the Academia and Press super-tribes. The likely cause of such shifts is meme pollution. The whole tribe has become contaminated by other purposes.

Religions

Declaration of class Religion

```
class Religion extends Tribe        {
 {set Purpose ='Get members to behave.'
//Attribute   Data Type    Comment
 Book         List[Meme]
//Methods
 Adjudicate(Chide) {...} // Weak punishment
 BurnWitch() {...}   } // Deprecated
class Sect extends Religion{
 {set Purpose='Walk this way!'}}
class Church extends Band { // one bldg.
 {set Purpose='Support neighbors'}}
```

No churches in the Stone Age

A religion, like its language, was once synonymous with a *People*. There was no "church" tribe separate from the people in the Stone Age. The memes of the people were tightly entwined with their gods, to the extent that the gods "suggested" how they should behave. The main purpose of religion is *still* to get people to behave. Religions expand with empires and often outlast them. They once had more authority to enforce their suggestions, including the High Justice (death penalty). These days, they can just bark at you or cast you out. Any tribe can do that if you break the contract.

Religious view of How the World Works

Religion also seeks to answer unanswerable questions of life and death, the people's origin, and "Who keeps throwing lightning at us?" [113] More important to the survival and prosperity of a people, their religion transmits many memes on how to treat each other. Religions have long been a repository for a people's social interaction memes. The Ten Commandments did this rather formally early in the Age of Empire. (The Written Word, in stone or not,

---

[113] In the BC comics, it was the Great Merciful Zot, an onomatopoeia promoted to deity

is one of the best Age of Empire memes. Printing and Money are among the best memes spread by empires, in that even "primitive" societies accept them. Those memes "travel" well.) Religious memes travel with empires, too. Islam did well. Whatever Genghis Khan worshiped did not, perhaps because he killed so many potential converts. The extent of religion in the Mongol's abysmal Xeno score is hard to know. It may have been a Nomad/Farmer conflict. That sort of war apparently encourages thorough ethnic cleansing. In Stone Age territorial disputes, the winners evicted losers as thoroughly, though they might absorb the women and children. Enslaving the losers was more common in farm-based empires. The religion of the empire does not much matter on the issue of slavery, so we can't blame religion for that. However, religions get full credit for human sacrifice memes. Some religions have a deity or three. A deity is a commonly held *model* of a more-than-human being. Some elements of lore offer advice on what *not* to do, based on their deities' bad behavior. Polytheists can have a lot of villains.

Big churches in the Age of Empire

Religious memes can travel with successful empires and might remain long after the empire dissolves. This was the path of Islam. Christianity, on the other hand, infiltrated north and west from the Holy Land, using poor people as the transmission vector instead of soldiers. Then, a Rome-based hierarchy emerged. That didn't happen with Islam. The emergence of the Roman Catholic Church as a separate political force was something new. A Country without an army is stranger than an empire without cities. (See Mongols.) In terms of the three ingredients of life, the political power of the Vatican came from INFORMATION, specifically the threat to a Christian King's afterlife.[114] As a political force, however, the Vatican has seen better days. They have survived but not prospered. The Catholic Church remains one of the most unique tribes ever in that it requires its members to practice celibacy. They completely did away with the *Family* tribe! No other tribe has managed that.[115] All classes of tribe will try to attract loyalty from every other tribe, including from the family. The Go West meme, supported by many powerful tribes, took from (Extended) Family. The Nuclear Family emerged. Marxists specifically state they want to transfer loyalty from the family to the state, which they claim is the People. That doesn't make Marxism

[114] Back when chiding meant something

[115] Perhaps a Cult or two but they didn't Survive(). Shakers are down to one church.

a religion, but that's the best bin for them in this analysis. Other religions are strongly pro-family.

Levels of Church

The lowest level institution that represents "the Church" is the Community church. It consists of people you know (mostly), which is far different from a social contract with people you don't. Local families gather to bond with good people and implicitly declare they intend to behave like them. The first focus of loyalty in what most people call "the Church" is local. There are also regional and international levels of religion, which each have their own loyalty measures. The local church works better than a Neighborhood as a support group for family tribes. The community church was the first African American institution to emerge after the Civil War. An Evangelical church is a new twist (a minor *emergence*). Television adds an audience lacking the personal contact resulting from physical attendance at the services. Coordination between local churches implies a level above, called a *Sect* here, like Lutherans or Shia. Above that may be a supertribe like Christianity or Islam declared as a *Religion* above. A member's level of loyalty to the church, sect, or religion are different. Religious wars need a "To Die For" level of loyalty. Conflict between community churches is rare but *Sects* and *Religions* might go at it.

Class Religion.Trending="Down"

Instances of class Religion had more power in the past. The Pope can't order a crusade these days. In the Middle Ages, the entire *Civilizations* of Christianity and Islam were in conflict. Violence has also taken place within religions, between Sects. How much authority is given to any super-tribe to change the behavior of its members? Do they have a Call to War? Physical battles between religious tribes are bad behavior in the liberal West. Other religions or specific sects haven't caught that peaceful meme. The Liberal meme means more than simply not killing the Other. Marrying one gets you positive Xeno points. Forcing her to join your religion loses you points. Religions and sects can have different scores on the Change axis as well. That's where most of the Traditionalists come from. There are also differences between sects in the extent to which the tribe expects the individual to Submit(). This places that instance of tribe higher or lower on the Control Stack.

Value Adding Tribes

Family businesses

With the Agriculture meme, our manner of gathering energy became less of a group (hunting party) enterprise. In the Stone Age, ENERGY (food) was *found.* In the Ag age, it was *created.* It fell on the Family to obtain ENERGY, rather than the Band. All sorts of new jobs beyond hunting and gathering emerged after the Ag meme. Such specialized activity centered on the family business for most of the Age of Empire. A Mom & Pop business is a form of Corporation now, an asset of the family, still. It's a tiny instance of a tribe that the family will almost certainly outlive. The tribe might outlive its creators if it goes public, but then it isn't a Mom & Pop anymore.

Guild declaration

class Guild extends Family[116] *{*
{set Purpose='Control the market!'}
Deny(Entry) {...} } // Can call the cops

116 Without the genetic intellectual property

A guild is a near obsolete form of tribe that emerged in the Middle Ages, as did true[117] robber baron behavior along the Rhine. The original robber barons restricted travel, adding no value. *Guilds* restricted entry into certain crafts. The Trust meme overcame the guilds, mostly. The American Medical Association, controlling entry access into the doctoring craft, is a late-stage guild. Guilds require access to state power; cities for the medieval guilds, the fifty state governments for the AMA. They can have you jailed for intrusion on tribal privilege. Board certification for other trades is guild-like behavior, but no other professional *Advocacy* tribes are as powerful as the AMA. Others are near powerless *communities*, who can chide and exclude. The AMA is not a weak community but an institution with teeth. Libertarian Milton Friedman was not a fan.

Corporations

The *Corporation* is the tribe that drives the Age of Plenty. After the Army, no other type of institution has had more impact on how humans live. The goal of the corporation is to obtain property and promises, often called making money. They do this by offering goods and services cheaper, faster, and

[117] Rockefeller and Carnegie were not robbers. They added value, in Age of Plenty style.

better than any other tribe. They stay in business by getting better at it. The network of local and international corporations that produce 90% of our needs and desires is the largest thing man has built, *The System of the World.*[118] Corporations are complex adaptive systems, as is the worldwide marketplace they swim in. The Market might be a super-tribe with a culture dominated by one meme, "Keep your Promises!" If you don't, you're out of business. No form of tribe has emerged that keeps its promises better than the corporation. Crony capitalists behave differently from "honest" capitalists because of their hybridization with government tribes. They found a way to avoid keeping their promises.

Corporate flaws

One problem with corporations is that they tend toward monopolies. Modern nations responded with antitrust laws. It just wasn't fair! This triggered a new tribal justice meme in the US called the Sherman Act. Nations have also added environmental regulations to handle polluters, another flaw in basic corporate ethics. Corporations are *not* incentivized to care for the environment. Both monopolistic and polluting corporate practices triggered the emergence of new

---

[118] A historical novel by Neil Stephenson, who blames the Dutch for the Age of Plenty.

Nation.Arbitrate() parameters. The social contract evolved to match the meme changes. The corporations weren't addressing the problem, so the Nation stepped in.

Manufacturers offer reshaped Matter, services save Time.

In terms of life's five basic elements, matter, energy, information, time, and space, *goods* involve (valuable) MATTER, but *services* don't. Services save the customer (valuable) TIME. Corporations strive to create such value using minimal ENERGY, but the key element of corporate success is INFORMATION. Corporations focus on the *processes* that create value. They stay competitive by improving those processes. Change comes fast among corporate tribes. No other class of Tribe needs to be so agile.

A Big Business tribe

```
class Corporation extends Tribe  {
 {set Purpose='Pay dividends'}
//Methods
 AddValue( )[119]  {...}          // And sell it
 Evolve(SOP) {...} }              // Techno-memes
```

[119] Replicated from family because Corporation does not inherit from Family.

Too big to fail

The need for a separate class for Big Business is stronger for companies "too big to fail." Members of this tribe develop high risk behaviors because they keep surviving them. They survive through government intervention. They don't have to pay for *not* keeping their promises. This is corruption of the main Market meme. The intersection of government power and favored corporations is a familiar place for dictators of famously corrupt regimes.

Corporate sizes

Small businesses conform to the basic mission statement of corporations, so we need no new class of Tribe here. Small businesses have no special powers. Cronies have a partnership with government entities, so they have resources and capabilities the little guy lacks. The crony's special power goes beyond Lobby(), which is every citizen's right in a Nation. Perhaps Crony.Lobby(Bribe) is the appropriate parameter. Big business (not just cronies) and *Bureaus* both benefit from the bureaucracies' Deny() function. Barriers affect small businesses more due to economies of scale, mostly in learning how to fill out new forms. Big businesses can afford to hire a specialist. Regulations tend to reduce competition from below. It's the philosophers of capitalism that love competition, not the practitioners. Also, if there are multiple regulation breakers, the wrath of the government is more likely to come down on the little guy. The big guy can afford better lawyers. Big businesses can get to love big government.

Leagues

Tribes can organize themselves into larger communities of similar interest. Universities form conferences to organize sports activities. Pro sports teams form Leagues. They have restrictive entry powers like a Guild, but that's not their main function. They are formed to *promote* (the sport) rather than *deny*. Their motto is "Play Ball". These supertribes have offices and employees who form a local instance of tribe as social, cultured critters tend to do. They specifically support justice. They monitor the behavior of their members and discipline any miscreants. The individual members (teams) submit to League.Arbitrate() decisions. The League has more than Chide() in its quiver, including Fine() and Suspend(). Therefore, they rank as institutions, not just communities. Bowling leagues, in terms of judicial reach, are communities (of class *Club*?). Social clubs have no salaried agents but have bylaws and refine them, so they are a tribe. Your circle of friends is a Swarm, a single generational group. You and your friends have a culture (of sorts) but are not a tribe.

Information Institutions

Most of the forms of Tribe mentioned so far deal with land and wealth. Land is the 2-D form of Space we crave. Wealth is mostly Matter but there is wealth in promises, too. Time saved is valuable and service companies sell that. Some companies sell Energy, too. There is no need to describe a new class of Tribe related Time or Energy. Information, however, is the focus of several types of tribes. Churches, for instance, are entirely based on ideas. Universities, museums, and libraries focus on information. Each is a local institution. Also of interest is the super-tribe of universities called *Academia*. Unlike a *League*, an association of sports tribes, Academia doesn't have an office. They are a *community* of professors with no real leader. But they do share memes. Institutions like museums and libraries are instances of tribe but don't have much of a super-tribe. The Press is a super-tribe of corporate tribes or instances of *Bureau* like the BBC. They once delivered accurate, relevant, timely Information. They have recently lost the handle on the accuracy meme.

Universities

Universities are an Age of Empire tribe. Scholars consider Plato's Academy the first university. In 1088 Bologna's leader (a *Prince)* established the oldest university still extant. The Age of Plenty has seen a proliferation of instances of the class. Universities are among the first tribes mentioned when the subject is Institutions. The US Census lists people in jails or mental hospitals as "institutionalized." So are students in dormitories. Each individual university is an institution, and a member of a super-tribe called Academia. Members share a snobbish meme unmatched since the days of aristocracy. Universities can be private or public, but this doesn't change their basic nature much. Universities, like libraries, exist to distribute knowledge. They also, along with laboratories, expand the knowledge base, pursuing knowledge for its own sake. Most labs are in universities or bureaus, but Bell Labs is unique as a corporate lab that shares what it learns, a behavior perhaps different enough to earn its own parameter.

Museums

Museums are another kind of "institution" that can also be a company or a bureaucracy. Is there a need for a museum super-tribe above and beyond the local institutions? Is there a culture that connects museums around the world? An Old Boy Network would seem to be a minimum to qualify for tribalhood. Does any group of individuals spend time in support of a museum tribe beyond their own local chapter? Is there a common meme that unites museum directors into a worldwide super-tribe? Is anyone paid to coordinate? Is there a specific location for storing super-tribal information? The case for an influential super-tribe is stronger for the press or academia than an association of curators.

The Press

The Press is a unique sort of tribe that the founders intended to provide a check against government excesses. It was not explicitly written into the US Constitution as one of the checks and balances, but it wasn't called the Fourth Estate for nothing. Individual press outlets are instances of the corporate class, unless they are part of the bureaucracy. In that case, they glibly support government actions more than they provide checks or balances. As corporations, they have a profit requirement that can overwrite the original goal of the press. That's how we get tabloids. Those companies provide entertainment rather than timely, thoughtful news on the state of the System of the World. Magazines tend to emphasize thoughtful analysis over timeliness. Newspapers have a need for speed. TV news has always been more cognizant of the entertainment aspect. The Internet has impacted all of them and changed the business model of many. A whole class of tribe can become obsolescent due to changes in the environment. The city found another reason for being after its walls became irrelevant. The Press may not be so lucky.

Bureaucracies enforce the Social Contract

An Age of Plenty Tribe

Perhaps bureaus began with Hammurabi's tax man, but the modern bureaucracy is an Age of Plenty construct. The Army is the country's strong right arm. It takes care of external conflict. The Nobility was responsible for misbehaving individuals and other issues of internal conflict in the Age of Empire. In the Age of Plenty, the justice function has been transferred to the bureaucracy. It now enforces the social contract for the Nation. It can put members of its own tribe to death. This was the High Justice in the days of the Aristocracy. The Army is the only other tribe whose members have a license to kill. The modern Western meme limits the Army's license to killing *external* miscreants (and deserters). Using the military for both internal and external malefactors is a bad meme but a favorite of dictators.

Hammurabi's code

class Bureau extends Tribe{// Do good (satire)
Deny(Permission) {...}   } // Don't do that

Expanding the mission, a bureaucratic specialty

The broad purpose of the bureaucracy is to deny the Country's members permission to do things that other members don't want them to do. Crimes are the most obvious no-no. The overall approach to crime has been punitive – after the fact–rather than preventive. The Bureaucracy began to Grow() when we expected them to take preventive measures, not so much for crime but for other hazards. This form of risk management has near infinite potential for bureaucratic expansion. The list of things the Country prefers you don't do keeps getting longer as the Age of Plenty progresses. We in the West are apparently getting more risk averse. We vote in favor of these restrictions. We pass bills in general terms, but the bureaucracy can fill in the details. There is little to stop them. The Bureau has few natural enemies.

Qualifying for a Bureaucratic Age

The Bureaucracy is a potential candidate for triggering a new Age of Man. The Army triggered the Age of Empire. The Corporation launched our current Age of Plenty. No other "artificial" classes of Tribe have had more impact on human history. Is the bureaucratic Tribe destined to have an equivalent impact? They certainly have an edge over other types of tribes, at least at the national level. The national bureaucracy of each nation has no real competition. A tribe's Grow() method is usually constrained by "neighboring" tribes of the same type. Armies keep other Armies in check. Corporations keep each other honest. The states or regions below federal control compete with each other, though less than armies or corporations. The California tribe is currently losing members to "libertarian" tribes like Florida and Texas. California is suffering from the excesses of Sacramento's Bureau and its unconstrained Tribe.Grow() method. The Washington Establishment is a similar tribe but is even less inhibited, since it's harder for citizens to change countries than states. The federal bureaucracy has been growing since the Depression. The question is whether it will grow enough to impact our lives as much as the Army and Corporate tribes have. If it does, we'll need to name a new *alt.age*.

Tribes for Our Desires

Associations for "other" purposes

The Age of Plenty has allowed other pursuits beyond obtaining our individual basic needs and defending the homeland from miscreants, foreign and domestic. We needed clothing and housing before the Age of Plenty, but those basic needs now come better, cheaper, and faster. Beyond those physical needs, we can now pursue our *desires*, those things that satisfy us. Those desires can be personal or collective, intellectual or emotional. The Age of Plenty provides our basic needs *and* the time we need for other pursuits. So, it has spawned all sorts of new tribes to coordinate the pursuit of our many desires. Our desires include anything important enough for individuals to commit their time, talent, and wealth to make happen. We don't get much chance to change the world as individuals. We get things done within tribes. Tribes have duties, so the tribes you support had better be important to you. You have several tribes to support and limited resources to distribute among them.

Supporting the Cause

class Party extends Tribe
{set Purpose="Win votes!"}
class Union extends Tribe
{set Purpose="Workers unite!"}
class Advocacy extends Tribe
{set Purpose="Change the world!"}
class Charity extends Advocacy
{set Purpose="Help them!"}
class ProfessionalSociety extends Advocacy
{set Purpose = "Help ourselves!"}

Advocating, what rich folks do with their time and wealth

The Age of Plenty brought enough wealth to throw a bit around. Orphanages popped up. This may have been an attempt to right a wrong that the Ag Age caused. Back when we were in the Band orphans were adopted, preferably by (extended) Family, but no child was left behind. Later, the vague "neighborhood" around a family farm was not so tightly bonded to that family. It would become worse in the cities, where the orphanage emerged as a form of institution, then died a tribal death in most of the West. This was a grass-roots movement at first, but the government has recently assumed that responsibility. Other forms of the Charity class have had more success. They went national and international and became nongovernment organizations (NGOs). Professional societies formed to promote their craft. Trade associations promote wealth generation in a non-specific manner. Unions promote their members' welfare in more than just monetary manners. They are not quite as altruistic as charities or other non-profits in the benevolent Advocacy class.

Neighbors, Once Close, Twice Distant

Neighbors back when

The hunter-gatherer band was the standard form of *humanoid* tribe long before we memed. The band is composed of (Kardashev level I) Family tribes who share anything they learn on the hunt or any other project with the (Kardashev level II) Band. After work, there are circles of friends and BFFs, but small social networks are not tribes. The band "owns" any culture that emerges from them, too. Everybody knows everybody very well in a Stone Age band. Family secrets are hard. (Family recipes are an Age of Empire emergence.) The other members of the hunter-gatherer band were more than Neighbors, as we now define the term. They were *comrades* in every collective endeavor. They had to be. There wasn't anyone else around. Our bond with our immediate neighbors was

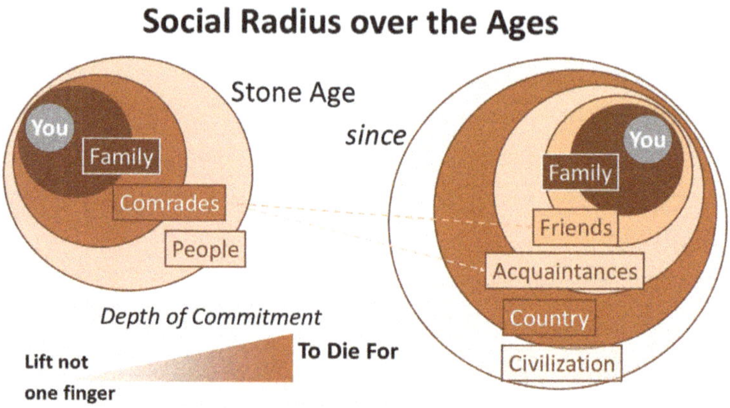

Making Acquaintances

never stronger. The "neighborhood" *is* the Band in the Stone Age. A separate tribal class called Neighborhood wasn't needed until the class of tribe called City emerged.

Acquaintances

We define Neighbors as those people you know by name. More specifically, they are people everyone in your family knows. In the Stone Age, that's the same thing as the *Band*. In the Ag age, there were suddenly too many people to know. A group called *acquaintances* emerged, people that you know but your kids don't. They and your neighbors still might form a support group, but a weak one compared to the commitment you might expect as a member of the Band. The level of commitment to the neighbors in the Stone Age Band was ToDieFor. Acquaintances never earned that level of commitment.

Urban neighborhoods

The Neighborhood (class) is a city tribe, composed of friends and acquaintances. It can have its own culture separate from the city. It outlives its current members. It ranks as a *community*. The bonds got weaker when *suburbia* emerged, to the point of nonexistence. The *neighborhood* has really gone downhill.

Tribalism

Tribalism, good or bad?

It is currently fashionable to label behavior you don't like as "tribalism." You can apply that label to religious, political, or other groups (They/Them). Some modern thinkers disparage patriotism as tribal, with a frown. Implied is that tribal behavior is not appropriate in the civilized world. Tribalism is savage, they say, and not the noble kind of savage. Sophisticated folk have evolved beyond that, the sophisticated folk think. Opposing that attitude, the argument here is that voluntary loyalty to a tribe is a good thing. You don't get much done by yourself. Only tribes do great things. They also do terrible things, but that's not the point. Your willingness to spend your life for your family or country is an extreme measure of tribalism. There are lesser fees that a member is willing to pay to stay in other tribes. Another way to define tribalism is the willingness to force *other* members of the tribe to sacrifice for the group. This tallies with position on the Control Stack. Authoritarians feel you owe much/all to the tribe. "The needs of the many outweigh the needs of the few, or the one."[120]

Tribalism over the Ages

Stone Age: Weak loyalty to the People

Voluntary commitment "to the People" changed as the Peoples of the Stone Age segued to Kingdoms and Empires and again when they became Nations. Patriotism is a modern middle-class value. The

[120] Mr. Spock eventually reverses the meme and now votes Libertarian.

meme changed twice. The willingness to die for one's people increased each time. The purpose of the Country is to defend the land that feeds the people. In the Stone Age, a people didn't have a country. They had an unorganized territory. A Country is an organized tribe evolved for homeland defense. When invaders attack a Stone Age people's territory, the people might run away and keep their memes. If they stay, they will have to fight again. That sort of thing builds bonds, even in the Stone Age. The most cohesive tribes are those that fight often. How often you fight depends on how valuable your homeland is and how aggressive your neighboring tribes are. The Barbarian meme pumped up the aggression meter. In the Age of Empire, aggressors came from farther away, more often, and more foreign. The size and frequency of aggressive interactions between peoples increased when barbaric behavior emerged. When the Empire first arrived a Stone Age people would often respond as a loose *alliance* of bands, a Swarm of independent chiefs with a War Chief. That meme proved ineffective against insistent barbarians. To retain their homeland, the people must adopt the tactics and organizational structure of the invaders. This included a permanent king. It also apparently includes, based on it happening everywhere, a two-class society.

Age of Empire: Fealty

In the Age of Empire, the peasants tilled the land owned by the king or emperor and his hierarchy of privileged nobles. *Fealty* is the term for that level of commitment to homeland defense. It is a stronger level of commitment to the group than an alliance, but not as strong as modern patriotism. One consequence of being "tied to" the land is that the king can find you. Hunters are, by comparison, "loose on" the land. It is easier for them to avoid the draft. Moreover, the individual hunter's primary allegiance was to the Band, not the People, unless the circumstances forced a War Chief on them. The Ag meme made the Band obsolete. Individuals transferred their loyalty up to the people-sized tribe and down to the Family. The family as a tribal form became more important in the Ag Age because farming families were not as tight with their neighbors as hunting families.

Age of Plenty: Wealth upgrades peasants to patriots.

The middle class emerged in the Age of Plenty with a stake in the game. The new middle class featured a more willing loyalty to the Nation. Patriotism emerged, an attitude a notch higher than the fealty a King inspired. So, from alliance to fealty to patriotism, the level of loyalty the individual members feel toward their homeland has evolved. Is there a step beyond that? Globalists assume we won't need patriotism. They are aristocratic fans of fealty and think that will work again.

Religious Tribal Loyalty

The level of commitment to religious tribes has changed. Few members feel a strong commitment to go to war for their church. That used to happen a lot and still happens in some sects. A religion that had the power to call for war was on a par with a Country. They would be downgraded to institution or community when they lost their super-devoted parishioners. The Pope and Dahli Lama lead the strongest *centralized* churches currently extant. Leaderless religious tribes can be "led" by Books. To the individual believer, church activity is predominantly local, in *community* churches. Their level of loyalty to higher institutions varies. Evangelicals follow a personality with no higher levels of churchdom. Jews are pretty tight with their far-flung (Book-led) community. They are the quintessential example of successful diaspora. No other diasporic culture has lasted as long, by a factor of ten. They have survived and prospered, so their memes must be strong. Judeo-Christian culture has many memes that helped in the emergence of the West. Other religious memes have other purposes. The Aztecs had a human sacrifice meme for terrifying and dominating their neighbors. That meme did not travel well, thank the gods. The memes of Islam were highly effective in the Age of Empire. Few cultures did Empire.Conquer() better. The Mongols (and Alexander) took as much land but faded away. The Roman Empire fell apart but many of its memes survived. Those empires were not as centered on religion as Islam, but Islam hasn't been an "Empire" since the Crusades. Islam does not have a central authority so is categorized here as a Civilization rather than an Empire. Is a Book enough of a unifier to drive a conflict between the Islamic and Western civilizations? We'll find out.

Tribal Fees

Life and Limb, or serious risk thereto

Only for Family and Country would you voluntarily give your life as an expected part of the social contract. As a parent in the modern world, you can save your child at the cost of your own life in a number of heroic and interesting ways. Kids didn't evolve to recognize all the dangers they face nowadays. Your country has memes for you to jump on that grenade. They'll claim you died for your country, but it was really for the guys around you, in your Band (platoon). Parents will accept certain death more often than soldiers. It requires a lesser level of loyalty to simply take a *high risk* of death for one's country, like enlisting in the army.

Time and talent

The commitment to institutions like a company or college will be less than life and limb. If you take a dangerous job, it's for the pay, so you and your family can Survive() and Prosper(). Institutions and communities don't expect much sacrifice. Short of your life, you offer your time and talent and, for physical work, part of the energy you ate today. How *willingly* members of the tribe offer their resources ranges from Slacker to Eager.

Good tribalism

The average Slacker score for all members of the tribe reflects deeply on the health of the tribe. Tribes have failed for less. Eager willingness to contribute to the tribe is the kind of tribalism that enables Tribe. Survive(). Tribalism of this sort is not a bad thing.

Memes

What memes aren't

These memes are *not* your cutesy internet sensations. Memes are to societies what genes are to species. They supply a channel to pass information from generation to generation. Memes are not limited to humans, but we're the only animal that transmits them using words and print and the occasional cutesy pic. The memes for "governing" human interactions are the focus here. We categorize memes for handling everything else in nature, living or nonliving, as *techno-memes.*

What memes are

Origin 1976

Richard Dawkins coined the word "meme" in his book *The Selfish Gene* in 1976. A meme does for society what genes do for species. It carries crucial survival information down through time. A good meme is an idea that helps a society survive and prosper. There are memes involving processes and many that require tools. The memes emphasized here focus on *behaviors*, on how humans interact with each other. Your behaviors half depend on your personal experiences (what you've *seen*) and half on your genetic disposition: Nature and Nurture. Half of your experiences[121] are not exactly your own. Memes that you've *heard* are basically the experiences of other members of your tribe. Meme transmission is subject to misinterpretation or memory loss, either yours or theirs...mostly yours.

The oldest meme?

One of the first memes of note was the Fire meme. This is a process/tool meme involving a new relationship with ENERGY. How this meme traveled is the subject of the movie *Quest for Fire*. Those tribes that caught this meme would surely divide history into Before and After. For those tribes, fire would be a Great Meme, a world-changing idea.

Of genetic and cultural behaviors

We know fire is a meme and not genetically inherited knowledge because there are tribes[122] that don't know how to start a fire. There was probably an Ember Maintenance meme before the Rubbing

[121] Following the 50% Rule. If you don't know the answer, it's 50%.

[122] mostly Band-sized, but among the Uncontacted tribes that band might be the whole People

Sticks meme. Most tribes took the upgrade. Words for *numbers* are also a cultural thing. Some primitive tribes don't have words for numbers, but might use their fingers or say, "a few" or "many." Thus, Numbers are a (techno) meme rather than a genetic capability, that is, nurture not nature.

Cultural backwaters – missing all the memes

Tribes without numbers (*anumeric* tribes) and dozens of other Uncontacted tribes caught few of the memes that have spread over the world since man started talking. They culturally appropriated nothing. Their strategy (meme/behavior) of minimizing human interaction has allowed them to survive but not to prosper. Prosperous tribes grow.

A most human ability: making memes

The Uncontacted tribes still sing and dance, jest and play. Those abilities are as old as mankind and genetic in nature. Talking is a unique capability of the human animal. Humanity began, according to one definition, when humanoids began to talk. Since then, only homo sapiens and their memes have survived. Scholars call man the toolmaker, but plenty of animals use tools. Man is the meme-maker or rather, the last *surviving* meme-making humanoid. Humanity began with the Human.Meme() method. We assume this includes Neanderthals and other members of genus Homo, not that it matters much. They're expired.

Memes without words (animals of culture)

Memes hand down the lessons the tribe has learned. Some of these are (techno) processes, like how to crack nuts. Processes are a type of information that can lead to a distinct culture. Elders can demonstrate some techno-memes without words, so animals less vocal than humans can have a culture. Non-verbal nurturing memes consist of distinctive behaviors the young can copy, helping them survive and prosper. Humans can't help adding words to any demonstration technique, so human memes tend to be wordy.

More memes without words (gestures)

Most human memes involve concepts too complex to demonstrate without words. Mama Bear may express disapproval of how you treat your siblings by shove, nip, or growl. They don't need complex communication like most human memes. Human non-verbal signals, even if they add to culture, are not memes, either. The Chef's Kiss has traveled well, though. The speed of transmission of memes across cultures is the focus of some meme research. Perhaps someone can get a grant to focus on gesture-meme travel (in addition to the proposed grant for animal-meme travel). But the focus here is on *verbal* memes concerning information critical to tribal survival, particularly memes on how we behave in groups. Gestures aren't subtle enough.

Processes communicate earthly knowledge.

The behavioral memes in focus here relate to how we interact with each other. *Processes* cover our relations with the rest of the universe. Process-memes communicate how we perform tasks. Their transmission method is the SOP. Father teaching son how to weave a fishnet is an early example. The continual improvement in our process memes is responsible for our current wealth. But these are things of earthly knowledge. The emphasis here is on how we treat each other.

Memes in disguise

Lore transmits stories for entertainment and moral instruction. Some are parables, full of hidden meaning on how to behave if interpreted correctly.

Stories are more memorable than posters when posters haven't been invented yet. Parables are stories with hints on how to behave, i.e., memes. The main impact of religion is getting people to behave correctly for the tribe to survive and prosper. Parables could be clearer, but all memes are subject to misinterpretation.

Memes as Vaporware

The ethereality of memes

The tribe has no physical mouth, so where do we get all those memes? We listen to Mom, for one. She's head of the Family tribe for most of the critters that practice mothering. Humans have dads to help. Dad also transmits memes for higher tribes; the band, the people, the city... and he heard it from his dad and so on. All of them were guessing.

If DNA is hardware, memes are far softer.

One modern expression likens DNA to hardware and culture to software. But culture isn't as solid as software, which is written so exactly a machine can "understand" it. Memes are even less concrete. Memes don't reside in any specific place. They are in your neighbors' heads. You filter what they say and interpret it within your model of how the world works. Memes are what you *think* your culture wants of you. This is one of your natural rights.

Your natural rights

From Mother Nature:

1) "You may **try** to survive." Critters or Groups. No guarantees. Watch out for Murphy.

2) "You control your actions." This natural right applies to critters, not groups, and only to brainy critters. DNA builds the instincts that control mindless critters. Many behaviors of brainy critters are written into their instincts as well, but they can make some choices. They control their own muscles; nobody else does. They have the liberty to chart their own path. Micro-critters, plants, fungus, and brainless animals just blunder into the future. Fish, at a minimum, can Choose() between left and right. Insects just Flinch() left or right.

Constitutional rights

America's founding fathers assumed the natural rights of life, liberty, and the pursuit of happiness. But nature conveys no right to life. It just gives every critter and group the right to *try* to survive. You have the liberty to pursue happiness, but that's just one option. The founding fathers elevated the goal "purſuit of happineſſ"[123] to the top three by mentioning it with life and liberty. The natural right of liberty is more basic and should rank at the top. Happiness should be one level down, along with other life pursuits like fame, wealth, hedonism, revenge, piety, or suicide. You can't pursue any of these things without the liberty to make your own choices.

Top level: Control your own muscles.

Nature allows every *brainy* critter the liberty to do whatever it wants. This is inherent in the fact that the critter moves and acts only on instructions of its own brain. Simple, brainless critters have less choice – perhaps none – so liberty isn't even on the menu. Even critters without brains will try to survive. That's written into the code.

---

[123] That's how it's written!

The primacy of choice

What brains allow is conscious choice. You don't have liberty if you can't make your own choices. Nature grants liberty to critters smart enough to make conscious choices–basically fish and above. Vertebrate.Choose() assumes every critter with a spine and a brain can make choices not purely driven by instinct. That leaves out the octopi, so we use Brainiac instead of Vertebrate. Carl Sagan called it the Reptilian brain. We include fish because fish are the dumbest critters that form mobs and can voluntarily leave them. We exclude insects as they don't go maverick from the hive, indicating they aren't smart enough to Choose(). Hives don't merge. Other kinds of mobs are more liberal on the Xeno scale with respect to accepting strangers (prey mobs more than predators, in general). Some insects have brains, but they are far from Brainiacs. Sagan would probably agree.

The origins of your decisions

Your actions depend on the decisions originating in your brain. There are four aspects to this:

1. Your instincts, automatically initiated by your brain (not by your genes directly, but

hardwired into your brain during its construction by your genes),

2. Your experiences, i.e., what you've seen,

3. Your memes–what you've heard, and

4. Your creativity, for when you can't find the right meme.

It's all in your head.

Technically, the memes you've heard are part of your experiences, but we make the distinction because this book highlights memes. The important thing to note about this list is that all the elements of your decisions are inside your head. Mind control is fiction. Your decisions are all on you. You can do anything you want, assuming it is physically possible. You can rob a bank. You probably won't, after considering the likely consequences, but you could. An important benefit of being a brainiac is having a risk evaluation engine that "argues against" robbing banks.

It's all your fault.

Even people in repressive regimes are free. If the thugs in charge say, "Obey or be killed," you can always choose death. You will probably choose to submit, and few would blame you, but it is still, ultimately, your choice. Nobody can reach into your head to make you move your muscles. All critters are free in this sense. It also means you are responsible for your actions unless you've been deliberately misinformed.

The true nature of memes

One simple definition of memes is that they tell you what the tribe expects of you. That assumes the tribe has a voice and, behind that, a brain. But the tribe has no physical matter, so it has neither. A tribe is simply an agreement among its members. We only *think* we know what society wants. We are born alone and will die alone. Every critter is a separate construct of MATTER. They have a sense of touch[124] that informs them of their immediate environment. Critters with brains use remote sensors to see and hear and have a mental model (the *Mind*) to interpret the incoming light and pressure waves.

---

[124] includes taste and smell. Smell is the long-distance tasting of chemicals from afar.

(Electro-sharks have an additional input.) Telepathy is fiction, but even if we could communicate perfectly one-on-one, we'd still need to balance the input from several people to make a judgment of what "society" wants. Hive-minds would fix this, but no thanks.

The Oldest Memes

"Run away! Run away!"

There are memes older than the Barbarian meme. One of the oldest is the Run-Away meme as practiced by tribes now labelled Uncontacted. Instead of interacting with other tribes, they fled. This can work if there is always a place to run. The pickings got slimmer as the world filled up. The peoples of the Run-Away meme now inhabit the most undesirable places on Earth. They have survived but not prospered, so by the measures of success promoted here, these tribes are only half successful.

Off the Main Sequence of human societal evolution

The Run-Away meme helped spread humanity into all sorts of forbidding environments. Some of those areas, deserts for instance, had exit routes to more productive lands that were worth protecting. Tribes readily rejected the Run-Away meme to settle down and protect these territories. Those tribes started the *Main Sequence* of human history. The runaways that survived were trapped in the worst corners. It was an early Stone Age social experiment, where a group of introverts led the pack coming out of Africa or the bottleneck at the Bering Strait. The Run-Away meme can't be considered a total failure. It may prove more survivable than following the main sequence.[125]

Stone Age Memes

Early ages of man

What might a caveman[126] consider the most important cultural changes to that point in history? Fire would certainly be on the list. In several branches of genus Homo, critters picked up sticks. Some species chipped at rocks. Those might be the Stick and Rock Ages if the Lore went back that far. The Stone Age as defined here started when people tied sharp things onto sticks. Lots of critters use pieces of the environment as tools. Some even trim

---

[125] That would be hilarious.

[126] There aren't that many caves. Most Stone Agers lived in the open.

a twig to make it work better. Man, if not the first critter to strap different pieces of the environment together to make a tool, is the last *surviving* critter to do so. Man is also the only creature still extant that talks and makes memes. We might assume Neanderthals and Denisovans had memes, but none survived. However, one of them could have started the Chef's Kiss or the handshake.

Early ages of Homo

Man is also the only extant critter to drape other critters' skins around itself. Clothing is a worthy contender for Great Meme older than Fire or the Stone Age as defined here. Humanity would still be in Africa without clothes. Migrating out of Africa has happened perhaps four times since Homo Erectus. Some of them had clothing. They would have had other tools. Tool use has been in the humanoid genome from the start. Clothing is a tool, and the urge to clothe oneself is probably genetic by now. The manufacturing techniques and styles (techno-memes) are pure culture, though.

Making tools and memes

The first meme needs to be more expressive than shouting, "No!" It needs a lesson, perhaps wrapped in a Story. It must become a *legend* for the elders to pass down. Which came first, memes or tools? Does it matter? Full-fledged "humanity" requires both. Homo Erectus may have had both. Jean Auel's fictional mute Neanderthals would qualify, using mime to pass memes on. It's not vocalization that distinguishes "humanity" but memes, even if mimed.

The Premier Stone Age Meme

Fire (making) would be a Great Meme for Stone Age people. They would have noticed a drastic improvement in their lifestyle. Great memes cause the greatest change in lifestyles. They would have a legend about how fire was found or gifted or stolen. (Says a lot about their culture right there.) The Fire meme represents a whole new relationship between man and Energy, one of the five basic elements of life, the universe, and everything. It doesn't get much more relevant than that. Our relationship with the latter half of Time is also unique. The emergence of new relationships with Information both started Life and started people talking. Language is one of mankind's premier *emergent* abilities. Fire making is one of our premier techno-memes.

The Dog meme

The Dog meme was a Stone Age emergence, the first of the animal domestication memes. It emerged as a new behavior involving another species for a purpose outside the predator/prey relationship. There are several purposes for dogs, each a different meme. All dogs come with an alarm. They can help with the hunt or guard the herd. Dogs can keep you warm at night, though it sometimes takes three.[127] They can pull sleds, another meme of the far North.

Flipping forward a few pages

The Husbandry memes are not part of the Agriculture meme. There are several memes based on our interactions with animals. Raising animals for food has the same purpose as the Ag meme, obtaining energy. Other reasons for domesticating animals get their own memes. There are several memes for beasts of burden, whether they carry packs or people, pull wagons or plows. The Egg and Milk memes involve food but differ from the base case in that the animal survives the process. The sheep survives shearing. On the other hand, the

[127] Source: album notes from Three Dog Night

Fiber meme (cotton/linen) involves agriculture for a purpose other than food.

Enter the Nomadic herder

The Dog meme is pure Stone Age husbandry. Other husbandry activities began about the same time as the early Ag meme, even if there were no farmers nearby. The Game Management meme emerged in the Hyperborean Age. It works for edible critters that form mobs like sheep, goats, cows, and (recently) reindeer. Horses have their own memes, not often associated with their edibility. Husbandry can work where agriculture doesn't. This gives rise to two very different styles of human culture based on farming or herding. We can further distinguish herding cultures by their pastoral or nomadic natures. There are different memes associated with these huge differences in the task of harvesting energy. In the animal world, new behaviors in energy harvesting lead to new species. Humans get new types of tribes. The vast majority of Stone Age Tribes were mobile hunter/gatherers. A few highly productive fishing spots allowed fixed populations (the first Hamlets), but fishing is just a wet form of hunting. The Ag meme forces a fixed residence, which is a far different lifestyle from hunting or nomadic herding. Agricultural land is always suitable for pastoral herding (dual use is assumed). The reverse is not true. Arid areas sparsely populated with energy-storing critters (Flora) can still support wide-ranging mobs of Fauna. A nomadic lifestyle in pursuit of this energy source is the usual solution. With a nomadic lifestyle comes a different set of memes, some involving tents. A more fixed residence is possible in rocky or steep lands with lush grass, leading to another set of memes for *pastoral* herders, some involving barns. Pastoral (rancher) memes are more like the farmers' than those of nomads.

The Boat meme

The boat has caused more species extinctions than any other techno-meme. Its predecessor, the Raft meme, allowed at least one migration to Australia, a disaster from the perspective of the big lizards that used to live there. More species would go extinct as man's ability to cross salt water improved. Rafts are not enough to qualify as a Great Meme of the Stone Age, even if the voyage was remembered in Lore. Their lifestyle before and after the passage was not much different. A meme needs more of an impact before we can label it a Great Meme. The raft meme does not compare to the Barbarian meme, which *ended* the Stone Age for anyone reading this.

Catching a meme

Memes can only *suggest* behaviors to a free critter. Memes depend on other peoples' knowledge, but not in a linear manner.[128] You get your memes from a *network* of people you hear (or read). You balance their words and perhaps integrate them with your personal model of life, the universe, and everything. If it changes your model and you behave differently, you *caught a meme*. Memes may be vaporware, but if millions of people catch a meme, they change history. The Great Memes changed how lots of people behaved. Twice.

The Great Memes

Alt.Ages, from the Usenet bulletin board

The standard three Ages of Man are the Stone Age, the Agricultural Age, and the Industrial Age. However, stone, agriculture, and industry are *tools*. Tools and tool-using *processes* are not the focus of this analysis. Rather, we cover the *behaviors* of humankind. For that reason, we propose the alternative ages of humanity, alt.ages. We'll keep the Stone Age for its familiarity. Alternatively, this

---

[128] Fortunately...linear information transmission leads to the game of Telephone.

could be the Natural Age or the Age of Savagery, depending on your political correctness. That would have included an earlier age when pre-humans found and used sticks as weapons. The Stone Age starts when humans or other advanced hominid species begin crafting tools. The Dog meme is the first animal domestication behavior. With the Ag meme, we started producing food instead of finding it. You don't need to find your dinner if you grow it or keep herds of edible critters. In the Age of Plenty, we create wealth instead of finding it.

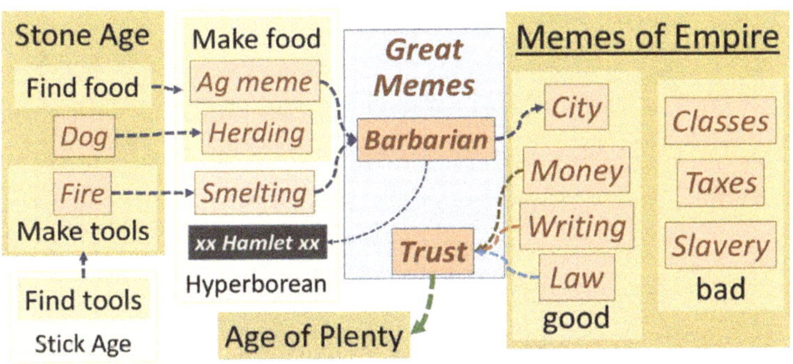

Memes of Note

The Age of Empire follows the Stone Age in alt. ages. We are now in the Age of Plenty. What caused these major changes in our lifestyles? The memes changed! Barbarians forced the City meme and fed the Empire meme. That spawned several major memes, some good, some bad.

The Hamlet: A failed meme

Agriculture began to make the Stone Age lifestyle of hunting and gathering obsolete perhaps 10,000 years ago. The Hamlet meme marked the first permanent human settlements other than a few hot fishing spots. The Barbarian meme made hamlets untenable.[129] The City meme was a more successful answer to barbaric behavior. City-states led to empire, and these have dominated human interactions for the last 5000 years. For some peoples, the Stone Age never ended, but Stone Age tribes did not get on the Main Sequence of human history. The Age of Empire isn't really over either, but the Western world has evolved beyond that. The Hamlet tribes went extinct as the result of bad meme. Other "bad" memes like cannibalism and human sacrifice might not have been fatal, but we're glad those cultures are gone. Of course, the main reason a culture goes extinct is location, location, and location.

---

[129] circa Conan the Barbarian's Hyperborean Age

Timing the Ages 50,000 to 5000 to 500 years ago

At an "order-of-magnitude" level of precision, we date the Stone Age to 50,000 years ago, and the Age of Empire at 5000 years ago. We suggest the current Age of Plenty began about 500 years ago. The Great Memes separate these ages.

The Barbarian Meme

Our most basic need: Energy (food)

The Barbarian meme is based on the simplest of needs: food. If desperate enough, Stone Age Bands would fight for food. The problem was that the target band, being mobile, didn't carry a lot of food. Stone Age peoples might fight for land but not food or wealth. The benefit-cost ratio rose significantly when farmers began to store a whole season's worth of food in one place. Historians might say that agriculture – the *production* of food – triggered the Barbarian meme and the Age of Empire. It would be more accurate to say the *storage* of food caused the ruckus. ENERGY storage is rare in the Universe. When it happens, the universal tendency towards complexity has something to play with.

Eli Wallach, that magnificent Barbarian

The Barbarian meme in its purest form states, "Our tribe can survive and prosper by raiding other tribes' siloes!" This was the goal of Eli Wallach and his banditos (Mexican barbarians) in *The Magnificent Seven*. All he wanted was food. Eli was a late-stage barbarian.

Upgrade to Empire

The Barbarian meme evolved in scale as hamlets scaled up to cities. "Pure" Barbarians don't try to possess the land. That is a separate meme of Empire tribes, which wants *control*, not just food. The Empire added other memes like tribute and slavery. The power behind the imperial throne and barbarians was/is the use of force. Emperors and kings reward individuals proficient in using force. They became barons, earls, and dukes. Nobles have special privileges not given to other members of the tribe. This led to the division of a people by class, a distinct departure from Stone Age behavior. A third (middle) class emerged after the Western world adopted the Trust meme. Actually, the concept of three classes is an artificial construct (like race). One western meme is that, ideally, no member of the tribe is "above" other members. We are a classless society.[130] The change in the number of classes, from one to two, and back to one, are *major* lifestyle changes for most of the world population, worthy of being labeled Great.

Empire Memes

The urge to dominate

The Barbarian meme led to the Empire as a prosperous form of land-holding tribe. The primary behavior of empires that makes them special is their Conquer() method. After the conquering is over, there are options in administering newly won lands. One classic approach is to Dominate() the local tribe for tribute. An older behavior[131] is to Evict() the current inhabitants and make the land yours. This is the most successful strategy, most recently successful in America and Australia. The conquerors forced aboriginal peoples onto the least desirable lands. On smaller land masses they pushed them off the island and into extinction. Little of the culture of these tribes remains, but conquerors take slaves, so the genes are seldom completely gone.

[130] The implementation of this ideal has been less than perfect.

[131] Territorial displacement of Mobs by more aggressive Mobs may have emerged before mammals.

Slavery under the Empire

Slavery is a meme of Empire. It became possible to enslave on a large scale. Stone Age slavery was limited to stolen women who eventually married the worst hunter in the band.[132] The band adopted stolen children more readily. Men could not be kept without feeding the guards more than it was worth. A society needs agriculture to be able to afford guards because of the economies of scale involved. Empires are harder to escape simply because they are big. They have mines, which are even harder to escape. Those are good for working former enemy soldiers to death. So are galleys. It is economical to get some work out of former enemies before they die.

Empire 2.0

With the Age of Sail, a new variation, the Remote Empire, emerged. Earlier empires were contiguous. None of them became "world-wide." With sailing ships, tiny kingdoms could become huge empires connected by Navies rather than Armies. Once they held a port, they could Dominate() the countryside. They could settle the land themselves or not. Latecomers to the game got poor pickings, so

[132] Aside from the shaman

German and Belgian colonies had few settlers. The Dutch and French had few emigrees to the jungles of Southeast Asia. Portugal and Spain had better luck exporting their culture, using the spread of those languages as a simple measure of success. The French got Quebec and some spare change. England got the brass ring in highly productive North America, a land inhabited by Stone Age peoples. Ag Age peoples like the Aztec are harder to Evict(). There are more Native American genes in Mexico than the US or Canada. England didn't try to replace the population and work the land themselves in India. They lost the Gem of the Empire in 1947. They kept America and Australia. Ethnic cleansing works.

The Trust Meme

A deep change in behavior toward strangers

The original Trust meme was, "Can I trust strangers to keep their promises?" It appears that we can, if the strangers are acting on their own self-interest. One significant group that bridged the We/They gap between strangers was Dutch middlemen. These were wandering medieval merchants who settled down in Bruges and Amsterdam in the late Middle Ages. They used mail as a substitute for travel.

"About" 500 years ago

Mail ranks as a significant techno-meme in allowing INFORMATION to travel with minimal ENERGY. It was one of several pieces that needed to be in place to kick off the Age of Plenty, like money and laws and property rights. The first stock exchange emerged in Antwerp in 1531. This is a fairly good candidate for the birthplace of the Age of Plenty, if we stick with the 500-year figure. But this and the 5000-year span of Empire are just "back of the envelope" numbers. The stock exchange and banks and mints and other institutions emerged and evolved over time. The Age of Plenty began to emerge *about* 500 years ago. It's a complex system. Things are fuzzy. Get used to it.

A new major Tribe

The premier type of institution to emerge with the Trust meme was the Corporation. No other tribe is as effective at creating wealth. The realization that clever people could create wealth separates the Age of Empire from the Age of Plenty. In the Age of Empire, wealth was *found* or *taken*. England took the new path. Spain didn't.

Release the Kraken!

To trigger the Age of Plenty, one of the ducks that needs to be in the row is property rights. In the Age of Empire, those come from the king or emperor. Most of the land was in the hands of the nobles. The fight between the Tories and the Whigs began when money became as important as land as a form of property. The successful king's variation of the Trust meme was, "Can I trust the commoners to get rich without my express permission?" This is a new behavior from the king, who grew up in a hierarchy. The top-down management style of the Army pervades empire and kingdom. The hierarchical tree can be a bottleneck. Releasing the hounds of "uncontrolled" commerce is akin to anarchy in the mind of a control freak. But Kings in Amsterdam and London and Tokyo[133] let the people loose and became rich.

The Birth of the nation

The Kings then lost their jobs, but that's another story. Several kings in northern Europe signed the Treaties of Westphalia in 1648[134]. These outlined

---

[133] Japan was a kingdom until 1874 at Okinawa. The (ancient) title "emperor" became legitimate at that point.

[134] "About" 500 years ago

the rights of sovereign kings, which segued into the modern nation-state. The Kings virtually wrote themselves out of a job. This is also characteristic of complex adaptive systems. New *emergent* behaviors aren't planned. They are often surprising.

The Money meme

Another of the ducks in the Age of Plenty row is the Money meme, an Age of Empire meme. Money is a promise in token form. "I promise you can take this token to the market and trade it for (whatever)…" It takes trust to accept that. Trust increased when the King minted the coin. Fewer merchants needed scales to weigh dubious gold pieces. The Mint is now a standard responsibility of the Country. Paper money redeemable as coin (promissory notes) took a little more trust. It didn't work as an acceptable payment for Anthony Quinn after taking Aqaba, for instance. With fiat money, the government says, "Trust me!" Printing a lot of fiat money eventually leads to a loss of trust.

Peace, for a change

The nation-state emerged from kingdoms or empires because those are the only choices. The Clan system is the only other "large" organizational form of land-holding tribe. Clans will have none of the Trust meme. The Nation is a considerably more peaceful form than kingdom, empire, or clan. Nations that adopt the Trust meme focus on trade rather than war. But there are still empires about, so many Nations are rather well armed. Some were once Empires themselves. The Viking empire is long gone. Modern Norse nations come from kingdoms. The Danish possession of Greenland was "found" land, so they don't (necessarily) follow the memes of Empire. Some of the Nations of today were colonies of empires, like the US and Mexico. Others were kingdoms who were late to pick up on the (naval) Empire meme, when the only land available to conquer was in Africa. Germany, Italy, and Belgium were the youngest empires and the worst at it. They have since given up their imperial ambitions. After WWII, all the western empires gasped their last memes and became Nations.

Barbarians still rule.

There are many members of the United Nations that have not adopted the Trust meme. They don't deserve the label Nation (in caps).[135] The modern version of the kingdom is the dictatorship, still

---

[135] We should rename the UN.

barbarian in nature and dependent on the use of force. There are still several empires about and a few old-style kings, who are slightly less barbaric than emperors. Modern monarchies with a figurehead king are *Nations*. Modern nations emerged first in western Europe and are still called Western, though adoption of the trust meme by Asian nations has rendered that label obsolete. The Japanese apparently had the memes for a high-trust society before the West entered. Some of those memes must have come from Shinto, just as Judeo-Christian memes underpin the behaviors of western individuals and their tribes. These are Ag meme peoples, where Islam came from nomads.

Migrating memes

Dictatorships are the Barbarian meme turned inward. The original Barbarian meme justified the use of force on the neighbors (They). That meme migrated inward to allow the modern dictator to use force against his own people (We). Similarly, the trust meme started by trusting individuals foreign to the tribe (unless you were Dutch), then migrated to the members of our own tribe. The newly trusted members were *subjects* of a Kingdom or Empire but would soon be *citizens* of a Nation. The nation trusted its Citizens in the juries of the justice system and in other aspects of the social contract between the Country and its tribal members. Outside the West, the world remained feudal.

A Quick Tour of Western Civilization

Conditions at the start of the Age of Plenty

Empires drove the major events of historical note. Kings opposed them. Both had a two-class society with an aristocracy lording it over the serfs. The lords were born to the privilege. Their great-grandfathers were the best barbarians. The advancement of knowledge was so slow it seemed life had been this way forever. The way to get ahead was to *find* value (gold being the best find) or take it from someone else. Cities were filthy disease magnets, but that was the fault of the city, not the emperor.

Middlemen kick off the Age of Plenty.

The first hint that wealth could be created, rather than found or stolen, came from Dutch middlemen. They got rich in a "poor" land with no gold or anything else to find. The King of England, then others, let their own peasants join in "the trade." The English colonies went farther in trusting the average Joe. In America, they replaced the King's law with middle class law. Nations emerged from Kingdoms (and a few Empires) wherever a People adopted the Trust meme. The number of wars started to decrease (slowly) as the empirical land acquisition meme fell out of favor. We started treating our neighbors better.

The Trust Meme migrated inward.

We started treating ourselves better. We rejected another imperial meme, slavery, though it took America two tries to give its slaves full citizenship. We gave women the vote, then careers. We even stopped littering. These new behaviors emerged in the West, where the idea grew that the average citizen was fully capable of making decisions. We trust random neighbors in our juries to make decisions of justice. The nobles once performed that task.[136] The power shift from the nobility to the commoners was a definite win for decentralized control, i.e., very libertarian. Societies that empowered the common man won the race for societal prosperity and (so far) survival. Kings and emperors fight with one hand behind their backs by not taking advantage of the talents of commoners. Trusting the commoners produced chaos, of course. The pace of change settled

[136] Colonels have the Arbitrate() function in modern kingdoms (dictatorships).

into the sweet spot at the Edge of Chaos. The West won the race...

...so far. Typically, human societal evolution finds one society succeeding due to superior memes, which other societies copy and refine. The Barbarian and Trust memes traveled best and had the most impact. The societies that caught those memes are obviously guilty of cultural appropriation. There is no natural penalty for that.

Analysis

How well have the memes of your People worked? What factors make a successful People? This section presents models of the factors that contribute to success. First, how do we define success?

Measures of Success

Of primary merit: surviving this long

The first and foremost measure of success for a tribe is whether it survives. Many of the tribes extant 50,000 years ago are culturally gone. Their gene lines are not necessarily gone. Genes would have survived wherever they spared the women and children. Some elements of a losing People might remain through them. Families might have "traditional" names. The last bit of the Lore they carried from the old days might be their name for the Boogeyman. These and their words for the local veggies, for instance, have long been part of the conquering culture's vocabulary. A string of mouth noises that model the object is not special. We all make models and mouth noises. A noise is not a meme. If all that's left of a People is a few etymological notations, those People are dead. Their culture did not survive the changes the world threw at them. No meme of theirs remains. Their genes are mixed with the conqueror's and don't count, culturally. This culture has passed on, is no more, has ceased to be, has expired and gone to meet its maker. This is an ex-culture.[137]

Live long and Prosper()

On the Main Sequence of human societal evolution, a separate People based on a distinct language would have emerged during the Stone Age. They spread if successful, i.e., they *prospered* in the SPACE dimension. They would have a territory, a language, and a set of memes for how to interact with each other. The memes would have been quite uniform across the world, as the only jobs available were hunting and gathering. There would be different

---

[137] If you hadn't nailed it to the perch, it'd be pushing up daisies!

tactics based on the local Flora and Fauna. Big game hunters followed the herds north at the end of the last glacial maximum. Some turned west and became Europeans. Some went east and populated China and America. An earlier southern route out of Africa got as far as Australia. Over the various migrations of man, hunters had already found the best hunting lands. People.Defend() memes were being tested at that scale to retain good hunting grounds. The Ag meme changed the definition of good land. Good farmland is not necessarily the best hunting ground. Where they overlap, the farmers soon outpaced the hunters. The Stone Age lifestyle could not compete with Ag meme population density. The farmers pushed the hunters off the most arable lands. In Europe, the Western Hunter-Gatherers met the Early European Farmers who had spread from the Middle East. Half of the societies that emerged during the Stone Age did not Survive() its end. Half of those did not Prosper().[138] The way for a People to survive and prosper was to catch the Ag meme. Societies that caught the Ag meme expanded into the land taken from the hunters until they met other Ag meme tribes. In terms of Prosper(SPACE), that people would have reached their limit. But they

[138] 50% being the least maximally wrong guess. Any other could be more wrong.

might have begun another phase of Prosper(SPACE) if they caught the Empire meme.

Measures of Prosperity: Prosper (Matter)

These days, the current owning tribes have already tied up 2-D SPACE on the surface of the Earth. Few Peoples are now prospering in the Space dimension. The Empire meme is not dead, but Nations frown on that behavior these days. There are other ways for a people to Prosper() besides gaining new territory. Prosper(MATTER) has been the focus since the Age of Empire. It was a golden age in that respect. We still measure wealth in gold. We can also measure prosperity by simple mass. We have *more* stuff now than a hunter could ever carry or a farmer afford. Mass quantities are possible due to improvements in the process memes that produce our stuff. Mass produced items are cheaper and made faster than crafted goods, though not necessarily better. The food is better, in terms of quality and consistency. Another definition of "better" considers the *variety* of products as a measure of prosperity. The Age of Plenty is better in so many ways. Success mostly involves better constructs of MATTER. He who dies with the most toys wins.

Prosper(Energy) and Prosper(Information)

In the Age of Plenty, we have more and better MATTER but also use more ENERGY. Energy usage is perhaps the easiest way to measure a People's prosperity, although it actually measures activity rather than wealth. ENERGY is a resource and an input rather than an output. It is a power multiplier that drives the Industrial Age. We use it to reshape and move matter on a scale unimaginable to a barbarian. They had just one horsepower or the wind for the Pirate subclass. INFORMATION is also an input rather than output to the system that makes us prosperous, though for some specialized tribes like schools and labs, information is the main output. How *much* we prosper from this information is very hard to measure. INFORMATION and ENERGY impact our prosperity invisibly, compared to the obvious benefits of material prosperity.

Prosperous times

TIME is another resource we parcel out to our various efforts to make our remaining time in this life better. Doctors and advances in medicine can add time to our lives. An aging population, however, is an iffy measure of tribal success. The pace of tribal evolution slows when members of the group have long lives. In science fiction, immortality generally leads to cultural stagnation. We spend time to get better times. It is both an input and an output. Every chore we do with better efficiency gains us free time. We work less to achieve the same level of wealth. Prosperous times mean more *free* time. We spend this newly won free time on individual or tribal goals. We can spend our time and other aspects of our wealth today or invest for tomorrow. Investing in future prosperity demonstrates the adult behavior of delayed gratification. That's a good meme for individuals or tribes. The other road leads to Hedon (worst case). Poor folk can't afford a lot of bad habits. Western success has allowed a wide variety of bad habits to flourish.

What do we buy next?

Western memes succeeded in creating physical wealth and provided options for spending it and, finally, free time to follow our pursuits. What have we been spending it on? In terms of the basic elements, we started buying land (2-D SPACE) as soon as the King allowed it. We bought higher quality MATTER in the form of better food, clothing, and housing as they became available. We spend more on tasty things from far away and softer cushions and other physical comforts that have become cheaper as the

Age of Plenty progressed. These derive from the SeekComfort() method that goes back as far as the Dragon brain. Purchasing high quality disposable MATTER is really buying quality TIME. We spend much wealth on quality fruits from afar to spend quality time through our taste buds. We spend more on INFORMATION than ever, especially in the entertainment division, which sells a good time. Vacations are way up in the Age of Plenty. The demand for vacations might plateau compared to vacations in the cyber-realm.

Collectively spent wealth

Citizens can also contribute to common projects beyond the operating expenses of defense and justice. The first expression of this was in the late neolithic with the Monument meme, which covers monuments to the People or their gods. Statues of significant members of the tribe are a newer form of tribal bonding. Statues of big things in general broadcast the power and unity of the People and enhances their People.Status score. The Cathedral meme added to many City.Status scores. The Stadium meme now does that for cities and the space race for countries. The Monument meme was an early example of the DoGood(Emotionally) method.

Measures of Merit

This is a term from operations research analysis. We strip an operation or system down a few key statistics that measure how well the system is doing. Societal "internal tightness" (from the Control Stack) and "external liberality" (from the Xeno axis) are two very different *Measures of Merit*. The Xeno Axis has seen huge changes in behaviors toward strangers[139], due to the Great Memes. The Control Stack ranks how we treat members of our own tribe, along the dimension of individual freedom vs submission to that tribe's social contract. There are other dimensions of togetherness, such as how polite or how cruel we are to each other. There are many behaviors that contribute to individual or tribal success, collectively, the Good Memes. We should make a list for Good Memes and another for Bad Memes. In general, we can rate memes near Normal behavior as good memes. Crazy memes are bad. In the Five-Bin ranking system, the two "eccentric" bins between normal and crazy are legitimate grounds for experimentation.

---

[139] Measured in *xenos*.

The Control Stack

The current expression of this measure is, "How much government would you like?" The answer places you somewhere on the left or right of the standard political spectrum. In more general terms, since the Country is just one type of Tribe, the question is, "How much freedom is the individual expected to cede to the tribe?" We could call this measure Tribal Power or Tightness.

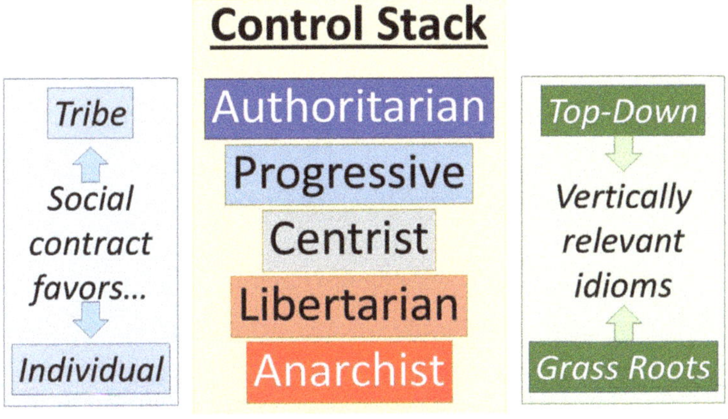

How much tribal control is acceptable?

The Stack vs the Spectrum

The standard model for the relationship between the individual and the Tribe is horizontal, expressed in terms of the left/right political spectrum. People who prefer more control are on the political left. "Conservatives" are on the right. Recently, American news networks have used the labels red and blue, which makes no sense at all but apparently emerged with color TV. Nonetheless, the Control Stack uses that color scheme. These colors are only slightly more arbitrary than left and right. The left/right model comes from a seating arrangement in the French Senate after the revolution. At least this vertical model has a couple of relevant English phrases in support of verticality. Top-down is a common term for a tight management philosophy. Grass roots is a purposely vertical phrase for a bottom-up approach, peasant rebellions being extreme cases.

The 5% crazies assumption

The Control Stack is a ranked list. It makes no assumptions about the population in each bin. We cannot assume 68% of the population will be Centrists. We can still *rank* them, so the anarchists and control freaks are still nuts. Libertarians and Progressives are just a little weird. A ranked list is a non-parametric statistic we use when we can't assume that the population follows a Normal (or any other) distribution. Non-parametric statistics are generally more robust (less likely to be wrong) because they don't try to be super accurate.

The Libertarian founding fathers

In the eternal competition between the individual and the tribe, the US Constitution is the biggest win for the individual in history. It is well into the Libertarian region in the chart above. People in authoritarian regimes accept huge amounts of tribal control over their lives. If it gets too bad, they revolt. This comes from the Grass Roots. We can map political parties into one of these five bins. On this chart, both major American political parties are Centrists. (We avoid using their names to give this chart a generic/international flavor.) We can judge any country on how tightly it controls its citizens. Authoritarians demand the members of the tribe submit to the tribe. Anarchists will not submit to any social contract that does not favor the individual. We could track how a culture changes over time. The US started in the Libertarian bin. In the 20th Century, it began ceding more and more control to central authorities. We are drifting upward on the Control Stack (or inward with respect to centralized power in a *polar* model).

An alternate coordinate system

Here we rotate the Left-Right model of the political spectrum to a vertical model, the Control Stack.

Vertical (the z-axis) and left/right are Cartesian coordinates. Polar coordinates are also useful in a political model or in social studies in general. They are the basis of the Social Radius model, where you are surrounded by your family, then friends, then acquaintances and strangers. Your circle of friends is a subset of all the people around you, though it's actually an annulus.[140] The We/They geometry is a circular *We* surrounded by *They*. So was the Aristocracy vs the Peasants or centralized governments run by "top of the stack" control freaks. Power radiates from the center in a polar model. Polar coordinates will remain socially relevant if we evolve to the InCrowd and the Outs that the World Economic Forum strives to achieve.

The geometry of trees and networks

In other network news, the King sits at the top of a hierarchy, topographically a Tree. He has Dukes below him and Earls below them. The King got this idea from the barbarian General. The Nation manages its territory through subdivisions (states/regions), and those divert some of the workload down to counties or cities. The hierarchy is a useful structure for managing tribal business. It works

[140] Please don't refer to your friends as your "annulus of friends".

best on well-known problems, like war. It does not handle *new* phenomena well. The geometry that emerged with the Age of Plenty is the *network*. You don't need to go through the bottleneck at the top of a hierarchy. Decisions are dispersed "to the field" (decentralized). This produces a faster rate of societal evolution. Such progress isn't directed toward any *dictated* societal goal. Evolving systems don't often go where they're told. The network of business contacts that grew from Dutch middlemen made us rich. Control freaks might support that as a goal but are uncomfortable with the method. The network is a Libertarian!

History on a Risk board

In the Stone Age, the "System of the World" consisted of independent Peoples fighting for the best hunting grounds. Barbarians changed the game. The negative sum game of *conquest* replaced the zero-sum Stone Age game of survival. The board game Risk is a fine model for mapping this stage of human societal evolution. The "System of the World" was led by empires, a central people that dominates other peoples rather than just kicking them out of their homeland. The agents in that system were Empires, Kingdoms, Clans, and a few Stone Age Peoples fighting for 2-D Space. The new *System of the World*[141] has corporations as its agents. The game is now *trade* instead of war. The West got rich by changing the game. The positive-sum game of trade now has more impact on our lifestyles than the negative-sum game of war.

Control Stack Trends

Chief of the Band

Excessive top-down control imposed on the Stone Age Band depended on the Chief's temperament, the Whim of the Alpha. The counter to that was the wisdom of the Elders, who invented customs. That was local politics in the Stone Age. Failure by both parties could lead to Chief.Duel() as the solution. In the Age of Empire, checking the King's excesses migrated to the Aristocracy. If they failed politically, a King.Duel() could occur. The upgrade could include armies. The Chief could only count on a few henchmen.

Control at the People scale

The Chief of the band represents that Band, not the whole People. A band member is tight with the

[141] Title of the Neil Stephenson novel that locates the start of the Age of Plenty in Amsterdam

Band compared to how much allegiance they feel toward their People. The people-sized tribe has hardly any control over the behavior of its Chiefs in the Stone Age.[142] Until a King emerges, the situation is close to Anarchy, the bottom rung of the Control Stack. Compared to the organizational structures in place today, the whole Stone Age was anarchy.

Age of Empire centralized power

Kings have more options to dominate their subjects than Chiefs. They have dungeons, for instance. They control far more land, so anyone who runs must run farther. Also, the runner may then need to learn a new language. The trip would be easier, with less hunger, for a Stone Age forager than a farmer. All these factors allow the King, as leader of the Tribe, much more power over members of the tribe than the chief of a Band. The average Kingdom is much higher on the Control Stack than a People, who don't have anything close to a central authority. We'll rate Kings as Normal to leave room for later Libertarians.

[142] Clash of Clans™ wars are a fine model for chiefs not listening to the War Chief.

Age of Plenty

The change from Kingdom to Nation is a Libertarian trend with respect to the opportunities for a member of the tribe to achieve *personal* prosperity. As the Dutch middlemen began to get wealthy, nearby kings made a choice: 1) to allow free trade or 2) keep system control close to the throne. England let the chaos happen. The King became a Libertarian! Spain rejected the Free Trade meme and stayed authoritarian. Both established huge remote empires, but English memes won. The English colonists in America tilted even further away from central control, especially in the Wild West. The cutting edge of the westward expansion was close to anarchic. Those wild spaces filled in with a "normal" crowd, who supplied enough social order to earn a Libertarian rating. The last bastions of anarchy now, aside from the Uncontacted tribes, are the various Clan cultures littered about the world in the wake of empire.

Inevitable progress

Since the days of the Wild West, the urge to impose control has led to more laws and more submission to the tribe. Is this inevitable?[143] Examples of a tribe willfully ceding control to its members are rare. All tribes want to grow. Most instances of class Tribe have limits imposed by other instances of the same class. Corporations, churches, and countries have competitors that restrict their growth. The limiting forces are weak for corporations. Monopolies are easy to create if an external tribe (the Country) doesn't step in. A *Bureaucracy* (the sum of all bureaus in the country) has no natural enemies. Bureaucracies in different countries seldom come into conflict. The force to restrict a bureaucracy must come from the grass roots, the anarchic portion of the Control Stack. Anarchists are not noted for their organizational skills. Things tend to build until they snap. Then a lot of tribal members go anarch and there is a revolution.

Techno factors

The options for top-down domination of the tribe over its members ballooned in the late Age of Plenty as a result of databases. Access to information enables centralized control. It could just as easily enable a distributed command and control system, but there doesn't seem to be an app for that.

[143] A ratchet seems the proper model.

The Xeno Axis

The Control Stack models a critical element of a Tribe's culture, the *tightness* of its basic social contract. How much freedom must the individual give up to obtain or retain membership in the tribe? This is an issue *internal* to the Tribe. There are also tribal behaviors related to non-members. These attitudes can range from xenophobic to xenophilic. Recall this graphic from earlier.

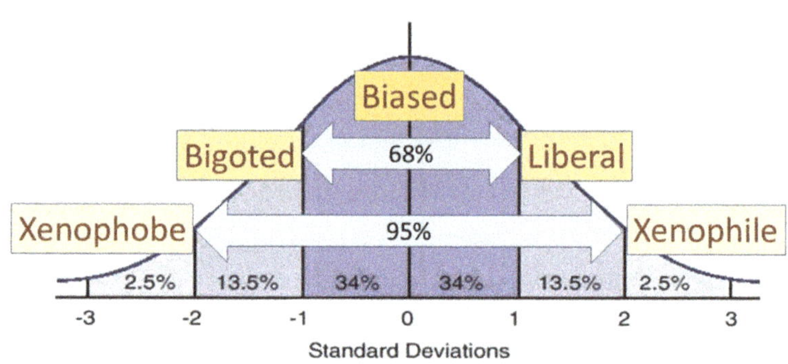

The Xeno Axis

Second of four metrics

This graphic is the second of the four tribal attitudes that drive tribal success and prosperity. First is the Control Stack. Second is how the tribe treats foreigners. We can rate individuals and whole tribes on their liberality. The survey is brutal. "Do you have special names for *Them*?" "Would you marry one?" A tribe's position on the Xeno axis can affect their adaptability. A xenophobic society might reject memes that come from *Them*. The worst case might be the North Sentinelese, who avoid memes that could contaminate their way of life by killing all strangers. Peaceful Uncontacted tribes just run away, which also keeps other memes of the outside world at bay. This may be more fear than hate, but here xenophobic can mean either. Xenophobes lose the best tool for improving their society, cultural appropriation. Most change comes from outside. The idea that Wakanda could develop an advanced civilization in isolation from the rest of humanity is, well, fiction (or fantasy, considering Vibranium's properties).

Xenophiles, loving thy neighbor too much

At the opposite extreme of North Sentinelese xenophobia are *xenophilic* individuals, who adore strangers so much (or their own tribe so little), they visit foreign countries and sometimes stay there.

68% of the population are "normal"[144]. In this case, it's normal to be biased toward the home tribe. Only Liberals want us to treat everyone the same, which is weird. Bigots are weird, too. Expats and isolationists are crazy.

Progressives are no longer automatically Liberal.

Note that this definition, combined with the Control Stack, divorces Liberals from Progressives, who are weird for an entirely different reason. The political spectrum tries to cram two measures into one word. Being "on the Left" means being Liberal *and* Progressive. There have been attempts to make a 2x2 mapping of Economic vs Social by Conservative vs Liberal. The primary purpose of these is apparently to obtain the rank of PowerPoint Ranger. A two-dimensional approach doesn't add much clarity. These are separate, one-dimensional *axes*. The Control Stack is a *ranked list* on the vertical axis. The Xeno axis is horizontal here, but you could make a vertical list. Combining them into a 2-D model is tempting, but it's just bad modeling. Representing two independent axes in one 2-D model has proven insight-free. It lacks good orthogonals.

[144] The definition of "normal" comes from "normal" people.

Xeno scores over the Ages

Stone Age (natural) position

We rate the Stone Age at zero *xenos*. Humanity has spent 90% of its existence in the "natural" state of hunting bands. So, we set zero as the starting point. Variations have occurred since. Barbarians caused a drop in mankind's average xeno score. The Trust meme made us more liberal. We could interpret the zero point with the probability that a Stone Ager would meet a *true* stranger with fear or fascination, 50/50. This would not be the case when meeting a *known enemy* stranger. Them you can kill.

Stone Age tribal interactions

They often warred in the Stone Age, using native North Americans as the standard for temperate climate tribes. Equatorial tribes *might* be less raucous. Polar tribes are far less warlike, being among the Run-Aways. Historians call the flood(s) of humanity coming out of Africa "migrations." That's the wrong word if its etymology is based on geese. Geese reverse course every six months. People leading the flood into the uninhabited lands outside Africa had no intention of coming back. Migration is still the wrong word when the land isn't empty. "Found" land is taken. Occupied land is *conquered*. Conquest usually requires war and armies. They didn't have armies in the Stone Age, according to the definitions here. They had swarms, temporary groups of critters with no institutional knowledge retention processes. If they didn't have "armies," maybe they didn't have "wars" either. So, migration is the wrong word twice. Swarming is better. "Noble savages" is another politically correct phrase that needs correction, if noble is associated with the Age of Empire nobility. Savages, without the noble, is more accurate than pejorative. In terms of a Xeno score, you would prefer your neighbors were savages rather than barbarians.[145]

The Hyperborean Age

Agriculture began in patches about 10,000 years ago. Bands settled down in hamlets. There are no strangers in bands or hamlets. That situation would change with the emergence of the city, where you could run into strangers every day. Civilized behavior required new memes for that, such as how to acknowledge a stranger without slowing down. We also needed new procedures for justice to replace the duel as the standard method of resolving disputes. The hamlet did not survive barbarians. Cities

[145] The savage who traveled with Dr. Who was nice.

did. Some became empires. City-states were a thing for a while. Most city-states merged into empires or kingdoms.

The Age of Low Xeno Scores

The Age of Empire is characterized by bad treatment of the neighbors, fostered by memes hostile to the outgroup. This behavior puts you in the Bigot bin on the Xeno chart. The effect of such memes is to emphasize the divide between Us and Them. Loyalty to the *City* was a somewhat successful meme early in the Age of Empire. People in the *next* city could be Them, even if They spoke the same language. The standard unit of humanity quickly settled down to people-sized Kingdoms organized to resist Empires. Members of a kingdom would (angrily) drift to the left on the Xeno axis as the empire kept trying to break down the door. You might assume the empire is more bigoted because they started it. But the Age of Empire was far from Liberal from top to bottom, though a vertical model isn't the best choice here.

Relevant dimensions

In more relevant dimensions, the Age of Empire was full of bigots from Near to Far. The other horizontal dimension is the province of left and right.

This is the x-axis in Cartesian coordinates. The vertical (Y) dimension has an unambiguous Up and Down. Left and Right are fundamentally fraught with ambiguity. Even mirrors can't get that straight. It is the only dimension you cannot communicate to an alien over the radio.

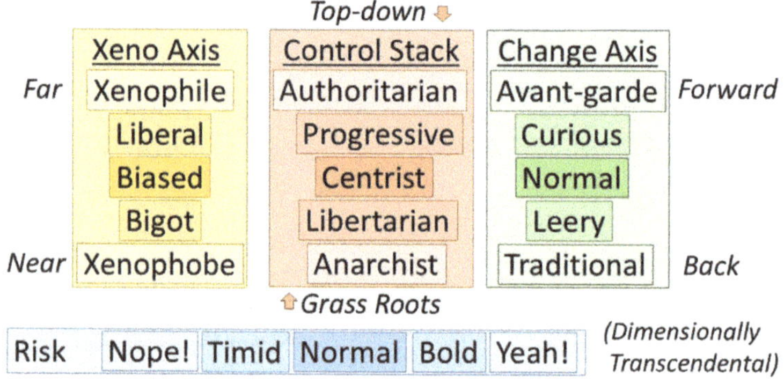

Geometric Models

We can divide the Z dimension into an unambiguous Near and Far (or Forward and Back). This is the scalar dimension in *polar* coordinates, which have a history in sociological models and idioms. Phrases like "Keep your friends close" highlight nearness in polar coordinates. On the Change Axis (next) Forward and Back are relative to TIME not

Space! The Risk axis (next after that) has no obvious geometric model relevant to time or space.

A positive swing

The negativity of the worldwide Xeno score in the Age of Empire has been replaced by a shift toward liberality in the West. Not all the Barbarians are gone, but the Age of Plenty is marked by much better treatment of strangers. Western countries have moved to the Liberal side of the Xeno axis. Over the last few centuries, religious tolerance began moving our Xeno score positively. We treat women better in the West. Discrimination based on immutable characteristic like sex, race, or age became illegal as the memes changed. Every change pushed our Xeno score up a notch. *Nations* are Liberal compared to countries run by kings and certainly emperors.

Inclusiveness

Modern nation-states are also more generous in who they invite to be part of Us. Recently, xenophilic memes have opened the borders of the West, allowing huge numbers of non-members to join the western tribes. They have not assimilated western memes and do not intend to. This may lead to trouble.[146]

The Change Axis

A dynamic situation

The Change Axis helps remind us that the clock is ticking. Everything's changing. Too many of our models are static. To find *trends,* we need movies rather than snapshots. Evolution is a competitive race. The pace of change is highest for societies that are leading the pack into the techno-future. How do folks feel about that? Traditionalists don't like *any* change. The other end of crazy loves change for its own sake.

A third measure of a culture's attitude

The "Left" should also include people at the opposite end of (conservative) Traditionalists. Here they are labeled the Avant-Garde, folks who might try almost anything. They're nuts, of course. So are the Traditionalists. Xenophobes wouldn't accept new memes from afar. Traditionalists won't buy in

[146] Ya think???

because they are new. Their meme is "Don't rock the boat."

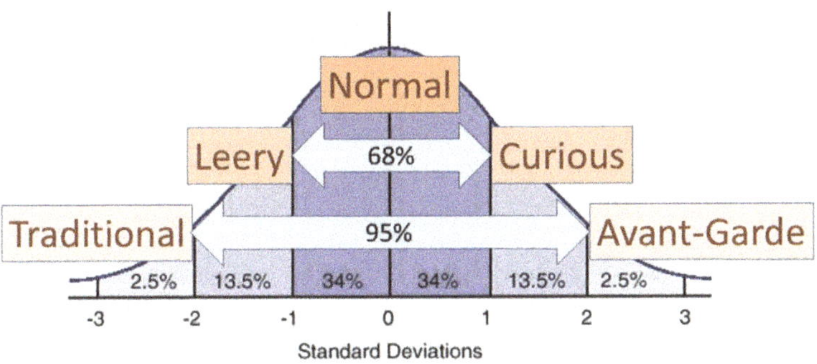

The Change Axis

Don't use the label Conservative – too much baggage

Note that Traditional is another word for Conservative. But we also hear of "conservative" investors, which is a potential label on the Risk axis (next). Conservative has other associations[147], so we decided not to use it as a label for any of these Five-Bin charts. We did manage to salvage Liberal as a label on the Xeno axis, but only after divorcing it from Progressive. We hereby (also) divorce

---

147 Conservative = Bigot, for instance, is unjustified. These measures are (mostly) independent.

Avant-garde from Liberal. Today's "Lefties" are a composite of three attitudes: Avant-garde change pushers, Progressive government advocates, and Liberal lovers of Others. But if the Left continues to insist prejudice against whites isn't prejudice, they'll lose their Liberal card.

Strictly an Age of Plenty thing

The Change axis measures an individual's or a tribe's feelings about societal changes. The rate of change was so close to zero in the Stone Age that the question isn't even relevant. The pace of change rose to "slow" in the Age of Empire. The conditions surrounding one's life were very nearly the same from birth to death. Farmers as well as hunters wouldn't understand the question, "How do you feel about the pace of societal change?" The Change Axis is an Age of Plenty phenomenon. There is now an expectation that "things" will change for the better, or at least they could.

The extremes

The Change axis ranges from Traditional to Avant-Garde. Whole societies are commonly called Traditional, seldom Avante-Garde, though certain cities might be. Paris was the first, but it was really a *community* within that city that should get the credit. The original "advance guard" was a French military formation. They were at the forefront of the action. Artists commandeered the term to describe their edgiest art. Things can change fast when society rewards novelty and continuous innovation. The fashion and entertainment industries have found acceptable niches. The faster things change, the better for them. There's fame and fortune for being in the community at the forefront of change for its own sake. Of course, they're crazy. At the other end of crazy are the Traditionalists. They oppose any kind of change, especially changes in the expected behaviors of members of the tribe. The rest of us range from Leery to Curious with respect to the willingness to change the rules of our social contract(s).

Trends in trending

The pace of change was zero in the Stone Age and linear in the Age of Empire. We've gone exponential in the Age of Plenty. That's not a thing *any* tribe has evolved to handle. We are getting into *Future Shock* territory. Toffler contended that the rapid pace of change in the modern world was bringing the future to us faster than we'd like. Whether we like it or not, expecting more change is an easy trend to predict.

Risk Comfort

Risky Business – The gambler in you

Another metric for rating a society is its attitude toward *risk*. How comfortable are tribes or individuals in taking risks? For individuals, nature imprints a normal distribution of risk comfort in every brainy critter. Sometimes, only the Bold survive, sometimes the Shy. On the tribal scale, Risk is the most volatile of the societal measures of merit introduced here. A tribe with its back to the wall will quickly accept higher levels of risk. They might jump one or two bins to the right in the chart below, if desperate enough, for instance at war. Risk is more of a condition of the environment than a deep mindset of a group. Some (crazy) individuals actively seek risk for the thrill of it. Few tribes act that way. They might embark on a quest that is risky, such as building an Empire, but they aren't taking the risk for its own sake. The modern trend, the Safety meme, is to reduce risk.

Risk takers

Individuals who are comfortable with risk go bungee jumping. They are bold, at a minimum. The crazy ones reveal themselves more readily than most other kinds of crazy. On a tribal scale, all barbarian societies are bold. The Vikings were crazy daredevils.

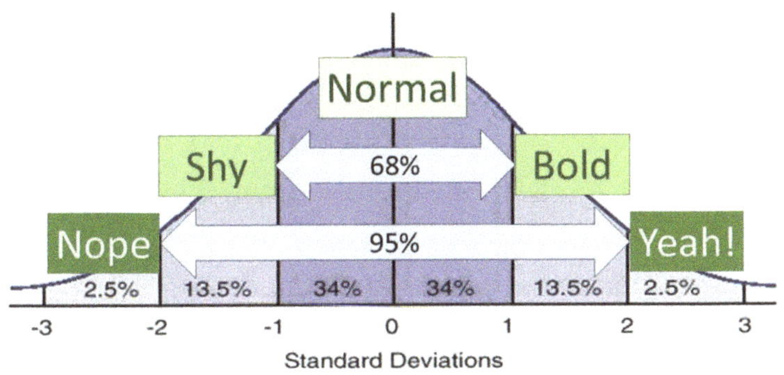

Five-Bin Risk Model

On the Shy side are individuals who won't go bungee jumping. The Uncontacted tribes don't see much change because they are xenophobes, not because they don't like risk.[148] Lack of opportunity to take risks on the tribal scale keeps them frozen, just as it makes them traditionalists. The Run-Away meme starts a with crazy level of xenophobia but affects the Tribe's position on the Risk and Change axes. We *assume* the Risk and Change axes are statistically correlated here. You would expect a person

[148] A Stone Age (barely contacted) tribe invented bungee jumping

or tribe Leery of change to be Shy toward risky behavior, rather than Bold.

Risk over the ages

The risk profile for Stone Age individuals was primarily to life and limb simply because they had few possessions to risk. The risk to a Stone Age people back then was loss of the Homeland to another people or rarely, a glacier. Droughts regularly affected a people's prosperity and sometimes survival.

Ag Age risks

Settling down to grow our food added our first major fixed asset, the house (or more realistically, the shack). The land may have been owned by the peasant or the noble, but every farmer needs a house. The Roof meme can be passed down by demonstration, so probably goes back as far as our simian days.[149] A house is not something a hunter owns (or defends), but he might build a temporary shack. A nomad can have a tent on his list of possessions. He probably values it as much as the farmer values his house but will have trouble getting insurance for it,

149 Chimps use big leaves for a roof.

even now. Homeowners were self-insured before the Age of Plenty. A house comes with a longer list of possessions than a hunter or nomad could ever transport. This includes the silo, an energy storage techno-meme that inspired the Barbarian meme. The nomad's herd is a more mobile form of energy storage and is less tempting for the Barbarian.[150] A farmer is more likely than a hunter or herder to defend a particular parcel of land. This translates upward to the People.Defend() task of defending the homeland. Certainly, the largest category of "lost" peoples are those hunting societies that rejected the Ag meme and lost their homeland. The farmers defended the land more vigorously just to save their roofs. They sometimes lost but still endured as a people.

The effect of Plenty

We stuffed additional wealth into those houses in the Age of Plenty...more to worry about and defend. Also, there are more ways to deal with risk. Insurance contracts are an Age of Plenty meme. There are two ways to deal with risk:

[150] But an emperor might want the land. Imperial armies are different from Barbarian armies.

1) reducing the probability that hazardous events occur (prevention)

2) managing the consequences if they happen anyway.

Insurance reduces the consequences if the hazard falls on you. Insurance became available for a wider assortment of risks in the West as we got wealthier. There are also specialized tribes that reduce the effects of floods and such, like the Red Cross and FEMA. Most Bureaus are on the hazard prevention side rather than consequence management. City fire codes are an early risk reduction technique. State and federal bureaus dedicated to hazard reduction now abound, reducing the probabilities of untoward events by denying permission to do dangerous things. It's a growth industry.

Safety culture

A long-term trend toward risk avoidance is occurring now in rich parts of the world. What do we do with that wealth? What's the first thing we bought when we started getting rich? What did a Stone Age denizen seek after attaining sufficient food and clothing? They spent some time amusing each other, so add entertainment as a budget item, logged under Prosper(Emotionally). We didn't have a shelter requirement until settling down in the Age of Empire. It's been a big budget item since, under Prosper(Physically). Food, clothing, and shelter are now The Basics. Much of our Age of Plenty wealth and knowledge go into improving the quality of them. We also have other options beyond the basics as we have piled up information over the ages. Our medical knowledge has expanded dramatically in the last century as well as our ability to pay for it. We are spending an ever-increasing portion of our wealth keeping old people alive. That's a growth industry, too, with a near infinite potential to absorb wealth.

Risk Aversion: Pining for the Island Life

An aversion to risk slows down societal evolution. It is a move away from the Edge of Chaos. We are shifting towards Island Life. The Safety Meme seems to gain converts as we get richer. We are also getting older and fatter. No society has ever been here before. We normally expect new behaviors to emerge under stress. Are these factors stressful? Is *ease* a sort of stress? Or is it a natural distaste for stress that pushes a society toward Island Life? Any animal is more comfortable in the absence of stress. Man is just the first animal that could do anything about it. We've made our lives safer on purpose. One of oldest of those memes is to eliminate our predators. Hunters would have desired fewer wolves and bears but didn't have the population density to succeed. Ag meme societies had much more success than hunting or nomad societies at reducing that specific hazard. Of course, farmers had stress-inducing barbarians to replace the wolves.

Genetics bets the spread

An individual's willingness to take risks is written deeply into their genes. Attitudes on the Xeno axis, in contrast, come more from the cultural side of the nature/nurture debate. The genetic variation of risk attitudes is good for the species or tribe at any level. Sometimes, you need risk-takers, sometimes only the cautious survive. We have a natural sense of risk. All brainy animals do. They have remote sensors and a mind that can interpret and integrate those signals into a coherent model of the environment. They have a memory that improves the model as experience tells. That's called wisdom. You can get wisdom from your tribes as well, as you absorb the experiences of others. (Budget item: We credit Elders with Tribal time for explaining their models of How the World Works to the young.)

Natural risk analysis

The model in your head recognizes hazards and assesses risks. In the Stone Age, the hazards came from animals. Barbarians changed that. Since Barbarians premiered, new hazards have emerged to threaten us and the property we have acquired. In the Stone Age, you carried all your property. In the Ag Age, you got a house/shack. In or near it, you stored a bunch of stuff you couldn't carry. In the Industrial Age, new risks to our survival emerged, in the form of hurtling vehicles, electrocution[151] and many new poisons. New risks emerge with "progress". But even with all these new risks, we don't bother to take our earbuds out before crossing the street. You just didn't do that sort of thing in the Stone Age. The modern human spends little time in alert mode, a habit we share only with domesticated animals. As fighter pilots would say, our situational awareness sucks. Add that to the list of consequences of modern life. We're richer, older, fatter, and less alert than any other people ever. Too many of us are *skating*, on the assumption that Death is far away. This comes from being rich and safe and a distinct lack of ambush predators in our everyday lives.

[151] Ignoring Zot's contribution

Alternative measures

There are other things we might measure, in addition to the four presented here. An analyst might investigate any "normal" human emotion on the tribal scale. Individuals range from Introverted to Extroverted in their preference for human interaction. Does a whole People (or a tribe of any other class) act like that? Individuals make their decision based on their emotions or reason. Could we compare cultures across the world by these measures? Individuals range from Rational to Romantic. Do entire cultures? Would such bins be useful in a Before and After analysis? Even if not in absolute terms, the trends might offer insights.

How are We Doing?

We can analyze modern Western culture and all its tribes in terms of the Control Stack and the Risk, Change, and Xeno axes.

Control Stack trends

On the Control Stack the USA has been trending Progressive since progressives decided we should do great things together. They are the source of many Nation.DoGood() methods. They favor centralized power and the Bureaucracy over individual freedoms. This is far from the Roddenberry Vision with its emphasis on individual achievement. Progressives want the tribe to do Great Things, projects beyond monuments to the people or their gods. (The Monument meme emerged in the Stone Age, long before progressivism.) The National Park system was a fine emergence. (But it has an underlying “Leave it alone!” meme that is *not* a normal arrow in the bureaucratic quiver.) Granted, putting a man on the moon was pretty cool as a collective endeavor. That will be hard to top, but there’s surely other progressive things we can do, like ending poverty. Apparently, the Charity tribes are insufficient to the task and the government, with its power to compel, is required. Progressives were able to change several memes toward centralized rather than dispersed solutions. The centralized control of the education system has the noble goal of equalizing resources and standards to balance inequities in local funding. Other increases in federal power include the finances of the elderly and everyone’s interactions with the medical community. These are the big wins for Progressives that have driven America higher on the Control Stack.

The Xeno Axis

The West has seen a long, slow trend toward liberality. Inter-ethnic marriages are on the upswing, for instance. Beyond Liberal (and crazy) is the xenophilic meme that all cultures are equally valid. Taken to extremes, this justifies human sacrifice or cannibalism.[152] Immigration is up, another indication of the Liberal trend. This can benefit the nation if the immigrants assimilate the behavioral memes of their new Country. If they don't assimilate; they are invaders, taking a piece of your homeland for *their* tribe. There is nothing wrong with keeping their songs and dances. And who doesn't like ethnic food, besides the Bigots and Xenophobes? Liberals and normally biased people find visible and tastable ethnic differences charming (mostly). You don't have to like them all. You probably won't like the music. That is a very nurtured preference. Accents trigger a genetic We/They reaction, but liberal memes can tamp it down. Liberal cultures tolerate all sorts of ethnic differences. Xenophilia goes too far, actually preferring strangers over members of the Tribe. That's crazy. Treating people exactly equally is at the boundary of Liberal and Xenophilic. The long-term liberal trend that resulted in the Civil Rights

---

[152] "The Aztecs weren't *that* bad."

Act has seen a recent reverse in three dimensions. Straight (1) white (2) males (3) get three strikes. The Left is no longer Liberal. It now promotes unequal treatment.

Trends in risk

America has been sliding to the left on the Risk Axis, away from a tolerance (even a veneration) of risk. We are becoming *averse* to risk. Cargo insurance helped kick off the Age of Plenty. Fire insurance came next. Life insurance reduced risk for the Family. Now we can get funeral insurance. Auto insurance is mandatory. Health insurance has become a staple in job offers from major corporations. The Bureaus have elbowed their way into that market in their efforts to DoGood(). That won't end well. Bureaus evolved to wield the Stick, not offer the Carrot. The latest market is for "sudden" car and home repairs. "They're inevitable!" True, but a bank account could handle that, and you wouldn't need to pay the insurance guy. It's taking more and more of our wealth to flatten the spikes. Another spike-flattening meme involves the Federal Reserve, whose ostensible purpose is to stabilize the boom-bust cycle of an uninhibited market. This is another example of preferring stability over chaos and pushing society out of the sweet spot for maximum evolution. Safety Culture memes cover more than insurance and stability. Helicopter parenting is another aspect. We are becoming more and more averse to risk. Shielding our children from risk is not helping them develop proper survival skills. Some of the risks they need to experience should threaten their lives (or seem to) if you seriously want them to learn to Survive(). They should go hungry once in a while, too. Nothing works better to properly prioritize the Survive() function than triggering that most ancient reflex. Desperation is a great motivator. Ask a survey question, "What's the most important thing in life?" How many modern citizens would answer "to Survive()"? The richer and safer we get, the lower that number will be.

Changes

The pace of change has been increasing since the Big Bang. It became noticeable enough to inspire *Future Shock* by Alvin Toffler. How we *feel* about change ranges from hate to love. The Avant-garde press for more and faster social changes that Traditionalists oppose. So far, they've gotten women the vote (and careers), obtained equal civil rights for ethnic minorities and gay marriage rights to a smaller minority. They are running out of minorities, but that's just the Liberal part of the Avant-garde agenda. They can still challenge the Constitution and other traditions as part of the Progressive agenda. They are on a roll and the Traditionalists and Libertarians that oppose them don't seem as organized, passionate, or ruthless. All they have is reason and civility.

Interactions trends

Interacting with others is a skill that takes practice. There are several trends in modern western life that prevent us from getting enough practice at human-human interactions. The American Dream describes a nuclear family living in an isolated house. This environment is several points removed from the one in which we evolved. We evolved to find food in a Band. Interactions between strangers were rare. Now it happens every day for city dwellers. We got used to it, supposedly. Then suburbia emerged and we ran away. In terms of the number of human interactions we experience every day, architecture matters. The isolated house of the American Dream seems designed to minimize interactions. The grass moat of suburban architecture adds to the standoffish effect. In contrast, houses abut in cities. Walkable cities are obviously nothing new. People interacted more when there were no cars or suburbs.

Nods work better than honks for positive Neighbor.Bond() interactions.

Grandma died.

In the Ag Age, the Homestead emerged. Family still included the grandparents and the odd uncle. The Go West meme aimed at the uncles. It caught Grandma. The worst part of this is the loss of Grandparent.Teach() opportunities. The Grands teach all sorts of lessons. One of those lessons is Death. Until recently, few kids became adults without seeing one of the four grandparents on their deathbeds. The nuclear family robs the young of that formidable lesson. Grandparents seldom died alone until recently. The Go West meme had costs.

Tech trends

Technology isn't helping. People with their noses buried in their phones aren't interacting with other people. Television (more than radio) started the reduction in face-to-face interactions. Movies, theater, circuses, and sporting events aren't as bad. At least you get out of the house. Storytellers are the original and most intimate entertainers, with the audience being a part of the experience far more than "canned" films or TV or other scripted shows. Sports fans can affect the outcome if they are loud enough. Most storytellers like a little interaction. Comedians actually like hecklers. If you watch a comedy show on your phone, you're doing it wrong. We can expect improvements in the technology of entertainment like virtual reality. Joy buzzers implanted in your brain, a staple of science fiction, are coming. The entertainment industry seeks to make your artificial life more interesting than your real life. That lucrative trend is hard to counter. They are selling you a good Time, better than you would have if you were physically interacting with people. It seems every new capability that promises to improve human communications tends to isolate us even more.

Is a new age in the wings?

We hear a lot about a New Age, sometimes abbreviated New World Order. There is a high bar for qualification as a new Age of Man. The change in how we live must be huge. We went from chasing our *needs* to working for them. In the Age of Plenty, we work for our *desires*. The most obvious new Age is simply the end of the Age of Plenty. "Back to the Stone Age" is the cliché terminus. The Post-Plenty Age won't be quite the same as the Stone Age because the Information we have gained will *not* be lost. We might lose the capability to do anything with that information, though. The most inevitable end of the Age of Plenty, if we get that far, will come from a lack of ENERGY. The oil will run out first, or maybe natural gas, and the U-235 about the same time. Coal will last about ten times longer, and U-238 about ten times longer than coal. Burning U-238 requires fragile "fast" reactors, but we *will* take that risk. A safer bet, and with 5X the reserves, is thorium fuel in molten salt reactors.[153] These could provide current power levels for 10,000 years. So, with some growth, we have that long to get thorium from asteroid 16 Psyche. Then we should be good for another million years. Maybe by then we can get hydrogen fusion to work. If not, we go back to an EROI ~3.0 using muscle power and ethanol. We can name that Age when we get to it.

Less certain ends

There are many world-changing (Age-ending) technologies in fiction. Genetically reshaping humans could certainly qualify as a new Age. Numerous cyborg scenarios would also qualify, up to the Borg meme. Artificial intelligence may be the nearest to technical realization. We might be uploading our brains into an alternative silicon life

---

[153] Warning: Soapbox topic

form. In fiction, many of these technologies result in a power elite of some sort, a new form of Aristocracy. Immortality scenarios trend that way. The overseers may be global or hegemonic. That will not much matter to the new peasantry, who the masters expect will serve the state. This is far from the Roddenberry Vision where the libertarian goal is to enable each individual member of the tribe to bloom. Instead, the tribe and its needs would come first. Collectivists win in those scenarios. In Roddenberry's vision of the future, they didn't. His meme emerged (somehow) in a post-scarcity economy. Given current trends, the Road to Hedon seems far more probable.

The ascendency of information

The power of information to domesticate the flock will be tested. The old aristocracy's instrument of power was MATTER (blades). A new aristocracy might wield INFORMATION as its preferred tool of domination (not giving up blades, of course). Governments have been keeping records for a long time, but databases are a significant upgrade in the tribe's ability to control its members. If this leads to Orwell, we'll have our new Age. If Orwell wins, the appropriate *alt.ages.info* might be Oral, Written, and Manipulated. The new system might have regional control, or it might be one global "empire". It might be Big Brother by himself if he's a computer. We will again have a two-class society of the powerful and the powerless. The In-Crowd would control the INFORMATION fed to the Manipulated.[154]

Unlikely Illuminati

There are many conspiracies of the Illuminati and such. Secret cabals are unlikely to succeed but, as was the case for the Go West meme, what if everybody's in on it? The current best candidate for global domination is right out in the open, headed by the World Economic Forum. The Go West meme worked as an unofficial "collaboration" with all the major American tribes, from the Press (not just Greeley) to the Country/Nation and its Army, all the Corporations, especially the bankers, and the Unions. Churches and Academia weren't really fans, but everyone else, especially the InCrowd, was getting rich. Is there a profit motive for enough institutions to support the globalism meme? Is profit the only unifying principle? What other memes could drive the emergence of a truly new Age of Man? Marxism hasn't worked nor has any other religion. The logic of Surak united the Vulcans, but we aren't Vulcans. Roddenberry's vision, "The goal of society

[154] But you didn't hear that from me. *anon*

is to enable each individual to reach their maximum potential", is not enough by itself. (It's actually just one line in one episode.[155] The back story needs fleshing out.) It is a Libertarian meme compared to the Authoritarian meme of centralized control in the hands of a few. The Roddenberry Vision abandons the idea that government should do great things for the capitalized People in favor of doing little things for the uncapitalized people, the *members* of the tribe.

Central control

Centralized control of many aspects of society is fraught with peril. The government hasn't evolved to juggle interest rates, for instance. It should not be surprising that they aren't very good at it. The Country has evolved to punish bad behavior, internally (Justice Dept/state/county/city) or externally (Dept of Defense). Authoritarians and Progressives want to extend their control. Essentially, they want to impose Newtonian control on an evolving system. They are never going to get very good at it. No one understands the system well enough. No one ever will. Unexpected consequences are the norm for those who tamper with complex evolving systems.

[155] Star Trek: The Next Generation, "The Neutral Zone", Season 1, Episode 26, aired May 16,1988

But that won't stop those Newtonians! We might take heart that they will eventually break the system and something new will emerge. A "new" version of Aristocracy is not new. It would not be a New Age, but the continuation of an old one. The Empire will return. A very few will enjoy that. The funny part will be that many of those who thought they would be on top will likely become part of the new peasantry.

Conclusion

In bullets!

- As an individual sentient being, you have a mental *model* of the world that you use to make your choices in life.

- Your genes and your memories built this model, including what you heard from your tribes. You have heard a lot of memes and Choose() which to follow.

    - You can always behave according to other memes. You know which ones.

- By staying in your tribe, you agree to its terms, oral or written. You have *duties*.

    - You will submit to the justice of the tribe.

- o You willingly contribute your TIME, ENERGY, and INFORMATION (knowledge, experience, talent, and creativity) toward achieving tribal goals.
- o You will keep your promises to members of your tribe.
  - □ Rules for outsiders vary. (A bit of Dutch trust went a long way!)
- o You have several tribes and owe duties to each.
  - □ You make the future better through your tribes, particularly *Family*, by providing your replacements with superior memes.
  - □ Your most basic resource is TIME. You can spend it on Tribal Time or Me Time.

- Tribes want to Prosper(), which often means Grow(). Conflict lies therein.
- "Normal" conflicts are competitions between tribes of the same type.

    - Asymmetric conflicts involve tribes of different types. Several tribes have benefitted by stealing loyalty from the Family.

- Tribes exist for a purpose. There's a list around here somewhere. Tribes can lose their purpose if captured by foreign memes. Fix this or get out.

    - Tribes can lose their purpose if the environment changes. That can't be fixed.

    - Complexity science emphasizes the creativity of evolving systems and their inherent unpredictability. Expect surprises. Evolving systems are not controllable like Newtonian machines. Attempts to control them cause disruption in other parts of the system. These are classic cases of the Law of Unintended Effects.

To Recap – in text!

Life is the most interesting phenomenon in the universe. It has two forms: complex *integrated* systems (*Critters*) that store and use Energy and complex *evolving* systems (*Groups*) that store and use Information. Evolving systems respond to the stresses on them in unpredictable ways. New behaviors *emerge*. The most interesting things in the universe are the emergences of new interactions between MATTER, ENERGY, and INFORMATION. Most of those surprises take place on worlds with evolving life, where new *Species* emerge all the time. The pace of evolution becomes supercharged when *Tribes* emerge within one of those species.

A social Critter sacrifices freedom of movement, and not much else, to the *Mob* to obtain the protective service provided by close association with similar critters. The restrictions on the choices of a *tribal* critter cover a far wider range of activities, especially when they talk. All sorts of behaviors become available for control by "establishing" tribal norms when we talk to each other. Different cultures prove their behavioral memes are *valid* by simply surviving. Tribes prove their memes are *superior* by prospering. The best prosperity meme that has emerged so far is the Trust meme that gave Western culture its dominating position. Western prosperity has led to material success, comfort, and long lives. This came from a dispersed network of independent decision-makers that emerged when it was realized that the commoners weren't stupid after all. They were capable of trust and responsibility, would keep their promises, and might even be civil about it. Roddenberry's Vision extends that trust in the inherent capabilities of individual humans, as opposed to collectivist dreams of great things done by the "People".

The problem is that prosperity can and has weakened the behaviors that produced the good times. A lot of bad memes have gained followers lately. Trust is hard to come by. Are we the weak men who cause bad times? We can take comfort that bad times will cause stress on the system and new behaviors will emerge. Complexity science says so.

Appendix

Tribes and their Purposes

Generic Tribe: (Goal): Promote the survival and prosperity of its members.

(Method): Transmit information to the next generation.

(Requirement): Arbitrate disputes between members.

Family: Raise survivable young.

Band: Hunt and gather.

People: Bind the bands in customs and war. The People is the repository of a common language, shared Lore, and standard behaviors. The People own a Homeland.

Minority: Keep the memes. Try to reform the Homeland or give that up and assimilate.

Army: KillPeople() and Break() things. The older martial behavior of *taking* things has gone out of style (method *deprecated*) as the Age of Plenty has progressed.

Country: Homeland defense and justice...same as the People but can raise taxes for it.

City (-state): Emerged to defy Armies. Now exists to maximize human interaction.

Empire: Dominate neighbors.

Kingdom: Stop empires.

Nation (-state): Do good.

Church: Change people's behavior.

Corporation: Make money.

Charity: Give it away.

Guild: Restrict access.

Bureaucracy: Restrict everything else.

Museum: Preserve knowledge.

College: Impart knowledge.

Library: Offer knowledge.

Press: Distribute knowledge.

Party: Win votes.

Advocacy: Promote change.

Union: Advocate for workers.

LifeSim Documentation

LifeSim Objects with their Methods() and *Characteristics*

LivingThing: A complex system that React()s to changes in the environment. All living things want to Survive() and Prosper(). They must Compete() to do so. Even the simplest species can Remember() how to build the next generation through RNA or DNA. The "smart" ones Remember() the past.

Critter: A LivingThing with *Mass*. It runs on Energy harvested from the environment and stored. It Eat()s until it Die()s. If it Spawns()s a worthy replacement, its life has been a success.

Micro: A single cell critter that clones itself, via Spawn(RNA).

Macro: A multi-cellular Critter that shares INFORMATION from two successful critters to maximize diversity, via Spawn(DNA).

Flora: A Macro of the plant kingdom. Has the Eat(Photon) parameter that powers life on Earth.

Funga: A Macro domain whose purpose is recycling.

Fauna: A Macro of the animal kingdom that can Move(). Excludes those lazy corals.

Brainiac: A Mover with at least a fish-sized brain. It has remote sensors and a Model() of the world in that brain. It has a longer memory than a gnat. The *Mind* is the electrical foundation of an individual Critter's memories and the Tribe's lore.

Warm: Animals that Nurture() their young: birds and mammals. They invented the first tribe, the Family.

Human: A warm critter that can speak and therefore Meme(). Also, the only critter that thinks about the Future and uses that ability to schedule meetings.

Group of Critters: A collection of critters with no mass (MATTER) that runs on INFORMATION. It extends its "life" via the Replenish() method.

Species: An evolving, involuntary Group linked by INFORMATION patterns in RNA or DNA.

Ethnicity: A subset of a species distinguishable by look, sound, or manner.

Breed: A distinguishable subset of a species genetically selected by humans.

Mob: A distinct subset of a social species with the power to call a Huddle(). It is voluntary in that its members don't have to listen. There are specialized methods for predator and prey Mobs like Pack. Encircle() and Herd.Stampede() that help their members Survive() and Prosper().

Member: A social critter that follows the Mob via Member.Submit().

Elder: A *tribal* member that can Meme().

Swarm: A temporary Mob–much less than generations-long.

Riot: (call it a day)

Migration, Rut: (season)
Marriage, Annulus of Friends: (lifetime)

Tribe: An evolving Mob, one with a *culture*. Its *Lore* contains stories, memes, and SOPs. The Tribe impacts its own evolution through its Elder.Meme() method. It also needs a justice system to Arbitrate() disputes among members. It has a *Morale* attribute that measures a key factor in a Tribe's *survival* and has a *Status* characteristic that measures each tribe's *prosperity* (in the eyes of other tribes, mostly).

Family: The oldest kind of Tribe. Not limited to humans. The Nurture() method helps their pups Survive() and Prosper().

Band: A small group of nomadic hunting families. Second smallest/oldest Tribe.

People: A distinguishable ethnic subset of humanity. This tribe helps its members by refining the memes that encourage members to act together effectively.

Army: The first "artificial" institution. Uses the Army.Kill() method. Strong right arm of the Country.

Country: Has sovereign authority over a 2-D patch of Earth. Has a license to kill both internal and external threats to the Tribe.

City: A smaller patch. No longer sovereign.

Empire: A land-hungry country with a Conquer() method. Gets credit for Writing (including written Law), Money, and Slavery memes.

Nobility: Privileged class within empire or kingdom with Arbitrate() and Punish() authority.

Aristocracy: Supranational, leaderless *community* of families linked by marriage. No authority other than Deny(Membership). Restricted to information operations like Chide().

In Crowd: Modern aristocracy testing the limits of information operations. Based on merit or old money rather than blood. Not a fan of the Trust meme.

Kingdom: The local opposition to emperors.

Nation: A middle-class Republic that caught the Trust meme.

Clan: A failed state. Not cohesive enough to be a "real" Country.

Civilization: Countries somewhat united by common memes.

Corporation: Tribes organized to offer valuable goods and services. They remain profitable by getting better/cheaper/faster at whatever it is they do.

Cartel: An illegal alliance of corporate tribes.

Crony: A legal alliance of corporate and government tribes.

Bureaucracy: Inherited the Arbitrate() method from the nobility. Can Deny() permission to do risky things. Tries to DoGood(). Wields the stick of justice effectively. Distributes carrots poorly.

Advocacy: A tribe formed to promote some non-defense, non-judicial cause, barely profitable enough to pay the staff.

Union: Advocate for the workers.

Guild: Advocate for a craft/profession. Its Deny(Membership) power includes government intervention, city (medieval) or state certification (modern).

Party: A political Advocacy that seeks to control the fate of the People in a legal and binding sense.

Universal Elements

(currently beyond the scope of LifeSim)

```
Time
Characteristics:
    Phenomenal=True          // Time is immaterial
    Direction="Forward"      // The Arrow of Time
Methods:
    Time.Start()             // Called at the Big Bang
    Time.Warp()              // Requested by Einstein
    Time.Warp(Stop)          // @ BlackHole
Child class:
    Event                    // A slice of Time

Space
Characteristics:
    Phenomenal=False         // It is really there!
    Dimensions=3
Methods:
    Space.Collapse ()        // Called by BlackHole
```

Child class:

```
BlackHole                 //Dimensions=undefined
```

Energy

Characteristics:

```
Phenomenal=True           // Until it touches Matter
```

Class instance:

```
TheUnity            // Quickly splits into
                    child classes
```

Child classes:

```
Gravity             // Causes Matter to collect
Electromagnetic // Everyday interactions
Strong              // To hold nuclei together
Weak                // To flip quarks
Dark                // Dark sheep of the family
Ra                  // Converts Strong to
                    Electromagnetic
```

Matter

Characteristics:

```
Phenomenal=False // The most real element
Phase=[Solid, Liquid, Gas, Plasma,
        White, Neutron, Black] // Star stuff
```

Methods:

```
Matter.Interact ()        // With energy
    Parameters: Melt, Freeze, Condense,
    Evaporate, Ionize, Collapse
Matter.Combine ()         // With other matter
```

<u>Child Classes</u>

Mineral, LivingThing

Information

<u>Characteristics</u>

Phenomenal=True // Vaporware

TimeStamp = {Past, Present, Future}

<u>Child classes</u>

Memory, Model, Promise

www.ingramcontent.com/pod-product-compliance
Ingram Content Group UK Ltd.
Pitfield, Milton Keynes, MK11 3LW, UK
UKHW021047100225
454900UK00017B/169